Dear John

As a lover of Sharpe and Master & Commander, I thought you would enjoy this antidote to tales of Imperial glory, along side the wise words of Terry Pratchett, which you already know well, for a bit of irreverent wisdom.

Merry Christmas Buddy
- Secret Santa.

52 TIMES BRITAIN WAS A BELLEND

JAMES FELTON

52 TIMES BRITAIN WAS A BELLEND

sphere

SPHERE

First published
in Great Britain
in 2019 by Sphere
an imprint of
Little, Brown Book Group
Carmelite House,
50 Victoria Embankment
London EC4Y 0DZ

An Hachette UK Company
www.hachette.co.uk

3 5 7 9 10 8 6 4 2

Every effort has been
made to fulfil requirements with
regard to reproducing copyright
material. The author and publisher
will be glad to rectify any omissions
at the earliest opportunity.

A CIP catalogue record for this
book is available from the
British Library.

ISBN (Hardback)
978-0-7515-7885-0
ISBN (eBook) 978-0-7515-7884-3

Typeset by M Rules
Printed and bound in Italy by
L.E.G.O. S.p.A.

Papers used by Sphere are from well-
managed forests and other
responsible sources.

www.littlebrown.co.uk

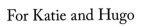

For Katie and Hugo

WELCOME TO
52 TIMES BRITAIN WAS A BELLEND ...

The purpose of this exercise is to bring together some of the events we conveniently leave in the shadows of history when it comes to our collective national memory, and to give them a thoroughly good airing.

The Prime Minister (in *Love, Actually*) famously once said, 'We may be a small country, but we're a great one too' and sweet merciful Christ haven't we banged that drum as hard as we can. But saying something doesn't make it true – luckily a concept that hasn't been lost just yet despite recent politicians trying their hardest to make us believe otherwise. This book won't ask you to ignore our finer accomplishments, but if you want to take credit for things our dead ancestors did, then I believe you should know all the other crap around the edges you're taking credit for too. Including – but not limited to – several massacres, our history of muzzling women and that time we killed 400,000 healthy pets in a week for no real reason whatsoever.

A few caveats before we begin:

1. The events in this book will be judged by today's standards. Most of the examples were horrific even by the standards of the day, but equally 'oh but I'm from 1612' will not be considered an adequate excuse for going on a massive racist killing spree.

2. Some of the examples in this book weren't carried out strictly by the 'British' – there are of course occasions when it was just the English being wankers all on their own, or times when the Anglo-Saxons decided to set the tone for the centuries to follow. But I am nothing if not inclusive, so if you made these isles your permanent home and were a gigantic bellend, congratulations – you made the book.

3. There are 52 stories as a sort-of-reminder that every week of the year we have the ability to be bellends. Sadly, the number of times we have been horrible wankers is not limited to 52.

4. This isn't a definitive history of the nightmarish atrocities we've done in our past. If you want the unvarnished history of bellendy behaviour I can recommend David Starkey for several reasons. What you'll get here is a good overview of fun and horrifying times when we were cartoonishly evil, from a comedian just as appalled as you are about what shits it turned out we were in our past.

Hopefully you will ~~educate your children with~~ enjoy it.

WE STARTED TWO WARS WITH CHINA BECAUSE THEY WEREN'T BUYING ENOUGH OF OUR DRUGS

There are many noble reasons to go to war. To fight fascism, for instance. To stop a power-hungry nation from spreading across the globe. To prevent an even bigger conflict from happening down the line. We started a war with a nation we were friends with – twice – because they weren't buying enough of our opium.

In the 18th century, China was pretty much the only producer of tea in the world. True to stereotype, we'd do anything we could to get our hands on the stuff. Unfortunately for us, China didn't really want anything we had to trade. Which is where hardcore street drugs came in. Say what you will about addictive precursors to heroin, they do sort of create their own demand quite quickly.

British traders, led by the East India Company, began smuggling opium they'd farmed in India into China. By 1833, we were smuggling 30,000 chests (weighing around 1,950 metric tons or 17 smacked-off-their-face blue whales) to a market of 4–12 million addicts in China. The Qing dynasty did everything they could to try and stop the problem, even writing to Queen Victoria asking her politely to pack it in.

Eventually China offered to let companies forfeit their opium in exchange for the tea. Unfortunately, our love of shipping drugs to a country with a massive drug addiction we'd fuelled won out. After China confiscated some of our illegal opium, we reacted in a measured fashion by launching a war to defend the interests of drug dealers against a country that had largely been a friend. It's like if Ross from *Friends* suddenly started pounding on Joey because he didn't want to smoke any more of Ross's meth. Yes, they aren't the closest of the friends in *Friends*, but it'd still make for a weird season finale.

Over the next three years the British government sent gun boats to attack key targets, leading to the phrases 'gunboat diplomacy' and 'God, the British really are dickheads, aren't they'. China, outgunned, gave in three years later. During the truce, we arranged better trading terms for ourselves and whilst we were there helped ourselves to Hong Kong, which was ceded to Britain.

And that was that, until fourteen years later when we fought China again for the noble goal of forcing them to make opium legal. So committed were we to get China to smoke more of our fine British opium, grown in let's say 'less than humane' conditions, this time we even teamed up with our natural enemies, the French.

In 1820, before the First Opium War, China's economy was the largest in the world. After the end of the Second Opium War, we left them with half the GDP and millions of drug addicts. But in our defence, we got quite a lot of Earl Grey.

WE MAY HAVE SLAUGHTERED THE VIKINGS BECAUSE THEY WERE TOO POLITE, SEXY AND CLEAN

In 1002, King Æthelred the Unready ordered the massacre of 'all the Danish men who were among the English race'[1] on St Brice's Day. The Danish had been settled in parts of England for a hundred years or more, so it must have come as a bit of a shock when they were rounded on and killed in notable numbers.

In Oxford, one group of Danish men broke into a church to hide from the locals who were in full pitchfork mode. Rather than think 'oh well, we tried' the locals decided the best course of action would be to set fire to the church, burning at least thirty-four men alive – on a religious holiday.

So why did this happen, and why were the (quite religious) locals so keen to kill a group of people (for which they probably believed they'd be damned for all eternity) that they'd even risk burning a church to the ground (and risk being damned for all eternity a second time)?

Well, as justifications for slaughter go, 'they looked prettier than us' is right up there with 'honestly we had all this gasoline lying here and I was bored', but that may actually have been a factor, according to one near contemporary account.

'The Danes made themselves too acceptable to English women by their elegant manners and their care of their person,' one 13th-century chronicle reads, justifying why the slaughter took place. 'They combed their hair daily, according to the custom of their country, and took a bath every Saturday.'

I know you already want to find their graves, dig up their skeletons and burn them one more time for this, but wait, there's more: 'And even changed their clothes frequently, and improved the beauty of their bodies with many such trifles, by which means they undermined the chastity of wives.'[2]

Yes, as well as bathing four times a month – like a queen or a high-end dog – these bastards were changing their clothes.

Essentially, we may have seen a group of well-kempt Danes and rather than deciding also to wash, thought it would be far less hassle merely to slaughter anyone else who did. Their cleanliness was making the rest of the English look bad and no just God could blame us for burning them alive in a holy building.

WE KILLED 500 PEOPLE IN 38 MINUTES THEN INVOICED THE SURVIVORS FOR THE BOMBS

On 27 August 1896, the British took part in a war that lasted less time than a documentary about that same war.

The Anglo-Zanzibar War took place when the Sultan of Zanzibar, Sultan Hamad bin Thuwaini, died. The British had a successor in mind, so when he was succeeded by someone else, who was anti-colonial, the British responded by getting all colonial on their asses.

Citing a treaty we had coerced the territory to sign, we informed the new Sultan that – by not seeking permission of the British consul to become Sultan – he had committed an act of war. Cue us immediately loading up gunships whilst Sultan Khalid bin Barghash hid himself in the palace. We told Khalid to leave the palace by 9 a.m. on the 27th or face the consequences, like a school bully offering you the options of having your money stolen inside or slightly outside the cafeteria.

Khalid, who let's be frank was also a terrible person and wanted to be free of the British in order to profit from slavery, gathered together a meagre army of 2,800 (mostly untrained) civilian Zanzibaris and gave some of them machine guns – I imagine a really bad thing to be let loose with on the first day of your job. Meanwhile, the British assembled three cruisers, two gunboats, 150 fricking *marines* and sailors, and 900 Zanzibaris.

At 9 a.m., the Sultan had still not left the building. Kind nation that we are, we gave Khalid a couple of minutes' grace and only started shelling the crap out of the palace when he still hadn't emerged at an unreasonably late 9.02.

Thirty-eight minutes later, the war was over as the Sultan fled for Germany and the flag at the palace was shot down. Five hundred Zanzibari men and women fighting the British had died, whilst on the British side there was a grand total of one injury from which the soldier in question recovered in full.

Defeated, abandoned by their leader and only barely not dead, Khalid's supporters left the palace, a sight so pitiful you'd have to be heartless not to feel sorry for them. Then, to really clarify that we were wankers in case anybody was too distracted by being bombed to notice, we made the survivors cover the cost of the shells we had used to kill 500 of their fallen allies, retroactively funding the slaughter of their own friends.

WE BEAT THE SHIT OUT OF THE WELSH FOR SPEAKING WELSH IN WALES

There's nothing the English find more offensive than foreigners in their own country speaking their own language. Just ask someone who works in a restaurant in Magaluf. And ask them in English for Christ's sake, it's the only way they'll learn.

This has been true for centuries, even though in days of yore we'd happily start a sentence with 'yea verily'.

In the 1800s, the English took over the running of schools in Wales. True to form, when they arrived and found that the Welsh children were speaking Welsh in Wales, they were madder than an expat in Spain who's just discovered their local tapas restaurant doesn't serve pie.

The schools introduced something called a 'Welsh Not'. If a child was heard speaking Welsh, they were given a piece of wood inscribed with 'WN' to wear around their necks. This could only be passed on to another student if they were found to be guilty of the heinous crime of also speaking in their native language. Kids were encouraged to rat on their friends, which is probably why to this day you have never heard of a Welsh mafia.

At the end of the day (or week in some generous accounts), whoever was left wearing the Welsh Not was beaten mercilessly by their teacher. Sort of like pass the parcel, but instead of a prize the winner gets the shit kicked out of them by someone trusted with their wellbeing.

The idea was basically to shame children for being bilingual, encourage a culture of snitching, and make tiny children associate their parents speaking Welsh at home with intense feelings of physical pain.

It was a massive success if you consider helping to kill off an ancient language because you don't know the Welsh for 'WELL, WHAT KIND OF PIES DO YOU DO?' a success. Which we do.

WE PASSED AN ACT OF PARLIAMENT MAKING IT ILLEGAL FOR US TO RETURN ALL THE SHIT WE STOLE

Whilst travelling around the world taking it over, you won't be surprised to learn we stole a lot of things. I don't want to defend imperialism but hey, you don't break into people's houses to *not* steal a lot of shit.

We stole the Elgin Marbles from the Parthenon in Greece, Benin Bronzes from Nigeria and Moai statues from Easter Island. We pinched so much from around the world that walking into a museum in London is basically like walking into an evidence locker with a cafe.

A century later, when it became generally accepted that stealing important artefacts for fun was bad, you can see why museums would be tempted to give those items back. As if seeing stolen items every day wasn't enough to make you feel intensely guilty, you also have to deal with countries phoning up every few days and saying:

'Hey, you know that massive stone head you nicked.'

[Looking guiltily at a massive stone head] 'Sort of.'

'Well funny story, we believe that's the spirit of our ancestors.'

'Oh right.'

'And we were wondering, since to you it's just a massive bit of stone to gawp at would you mind giving it back now please?'

The indigenous Rapa Nui islanders do believe this, and have asked regularly from the 1950s till 2018 for the heads at Easter Island to be returned to them precisely for this very reason.

In 1963, in response to a lot of ungrateful countries having the cheek of asking for their stuff back, we passed the British Museum Act, forbidding the British Museum from returning any of its holding, except in a small number of 'special circumstances'. This basically forbade the museum from returning the Elgin Marbles or the Benin Bronzes without a whole new act of Parliament letting them do so.

So when someone calls up to point out that we're akin to the villains from *Indiana Jones* and ask for their stuff back, we can tell them, 'you do realise you're asking me to break the law, don't you?' And then laugh silently into our cups of tea, 'who's the bellend now?'

WE CAUSED A FAMINE THAT KILLED MORE THAN THREE MILLION PEOPLE

If at the end of *Superman*, Superman flew in and defeated Lex Luthor – thus saving Earth – and then turned around and started twatting orphans with his super-strength alien fists, I guarantee there would be at least a few articles written along the lines of, 'ok bravo for saving the planet, but I think we need to talk about how Superman was a bit of a mixed bag.'

Well, Churchill – one of Britain's greatest heroes, who stood up to Hitler and won (with the help of many allies) – also caused the death of three million people in India*, and we should probably acknowledge that a bit.

In 1943, famine was sweeping through India, still one of Britain's colonies at the time. The situation was dire. People were dying in their millions. Parents dumped the bodies of their starved children into rivers and took their own lives by jumping in front of trains. There were reports of dogs eating the dead in the villages of Bengal. Yet during this time, under instruction from the British, India exported more than 70,000 tonnes of rice to Britain, which could have kept around 400,000 people alive for a year.

Officials in India requested several times that food be imported *towards* the millions of starving people rather than away from them, but were denied by Churchill on most occasions, or given a tiny amount of what they asked for. Accounts at the time from Field Marshal Sir Archibald Wavell say that Churchill thought that giving food to 'already underfed Bengalis is less serious than [giving it to] sturdy Greeks'[3]. I.e. why would we give it to millions of Indian people who are quite hungry anyway, when we could be giving it to Europeans who are already well-fed enough to be buff.

We even stockpiled food from other countries that we didn't need yet. Rather than divert it to deal with the crisis in one of our colonies where millions were starving, Churchill allowed food imported from Australia to sail right on past India to be stored in Europe. Like hearing an ice-cream truck go by when you're hungry, except you're starting to get a feeling that the truck driver might be a massive racist. Mr Whippy seems to be happy to stop for all the European kids, that's all I'm saying.

Food prices in India shot up as a result of fewer imports, and hoarders took advantage, stockpiling and shooting the prices up even higher, making food unaffordable for the millions of poor. Sadly (for the Indian people in the 1940s, and our current national pride) it gets worse. Historian Madhusree Mukerjee writes[4] that Churchill operated a scorched earth policy – in order to make sure supplies in India were low and transport was not around if Japan were to invade Bengal. Under this policy, rice deemed 'surplus' would be thrown in the water, and boats were confiscated from fishermen, killing the local fishing industry – which would have been quite useful considering there was no food. In essence, we starved and bankrupted a lot of Indian people, to starve the Japanese in a hypothetical scenario that never happened.

It would be easier to dismiss this as a grave mistake by Churchill or a tactical error had he not once said, 'I hate Indians. They are a beastly people with a beastly religion.'[5] Which even if you hadn't let millions of people starve to death is not a great look.

I know, I know: Churchill is a national hero, and people feel that by attacking Churchill, somehow you attack our own national sense of identity. But does it really diminish the good stuff he did if you caveat it 'apart from all the ruthless fucking murder by omission, Churchill was ok'?

He actually did some other bad things too, but let's leave it there for today.

WE BROUGHT AN ELEPHANT TO ENGLAND, MADE IT LIVE IN THE TOWER OF LONDON WITH A POLAR BEAR AND GOT IT WANKERED ON WINE

In the 13th century we decided to rebrand Britain's most famous torture chamber, prison and site of execution as a zoo. During the reign of King John, we stopped merely using the Tower of London to torture inconvenient royals with possible claims to the throne, and started also using it as an inappropriate home for all kinds of exotic animals. We kept:

Lions

When you see the natural habitat of lions – the plains of Africa – your first thought probably isn't that it bears a striking resemblance to a castle in England during the drizzle. Nevertheless, at several points in history the Tower was rammed full of lions who were allowed outside only during the day. Things improved down the line under James I when they got more 'exercise', by which of course I mean they were forced to fight dogs for the King's enjoyment. The King watched from a special viewing platform he had built to watch the lion fights with money he could have used to build some sort of lion play area.

Polar bear

A gift from King Haakon of Norway in 1252, the polar bear was allowed to swim in the Thames by Henry III, which must have been quite the mindfuck for the fish. It wasn't done out of kindness though; Henry just didn't like how expensive it was to feed a fully grown polar bear, which is about number 12 on the Big List Of Reasons You Don't Accept A Fucking Polar Bear As A Gift In The First Place, right below 'it's a fucking polar bear, why not try a rabbit first and see how you get on'.

The polar bear was allowed to fish in the Thames for its own food (whilst attached to a rope). Bearing in mind how grim the Thames was back then without a sewer system, this is like buying a puppy and instead of feeding it Pedigree Chum, making it hunt for rats in a toilet.

Elephants

In 1623, the King of Spain gave King James I an elephant and very little instruction whatsoever. This ended up with the elephant being fed a diet exclusively of various types of meat, mainly steak – elephants, if you didn't know, are famously herbivorous. Fortunately it probably didn't find this too distressing due to the fact the zookeepers also got it pissed up on an actual gallon of wine a day from April to September, believing it to be unable to drink water during these months and lacking the imagination to try offering squash.

Ostrich

To complete the menagerie there were also some ostriches roaming around, who again, we had fuck-all clue about and didn't bother to do any research whatsoever as to how to look after them. Don't ask me why, but someone clever thought that ostriches could eat metal, and so, even though we also thought they could eat actual food, the ostriches kept in the Tower were fed quite a lot of nails. This seems especially unfair when you remember the elephants were eating fine sirloin steak whilst getting wankered on Château-du-Pape.

WE SLAUGHTERED 400,000 HEALTHY PUPPIES AND KITTENS IN LESS THAN A WEEK

In the first week of September 1939, in those last lazy days of summer, Londoners set about systematically murdering 400,000 puppies and kittens.

Worried about scarce resources during the oncoming war, the National Air Raid Precautions Animals Committee advised London residents to send their pets to the countryside, or if that wasn't an option, to have them destroyed. Before you could say 'but this is purely advisory and you're not under any obligation to actually carry it out' the Great Pet Massacre of 1939 had begun.

We patiently queued up (God love us: we play to our stereotypes even during mass acts of pet murder) outside animal shelters, waiting our turn to have our beloved cats and dogs executed. Work carried on through the night. There was a queue outside one vets over half a mile long. Imagine being a dog in that queue, thinking 'A lot of these puppers aren't coming back out again, huh. Sure do love my owner though, bet he's organised something fun.'

It got to the point that crematoriums couldn't burn the bodies fast enough, and animal welfare societies ran out of chloroform to murder dogs with, because of all the dog murder. In just four days, before a bomb had even dropped, over a quarter of London's pets were dead. They outnumber the human civilians in London that were killed during the entire war by six to one.

And I know you're thinking 'it was the kindest thing for them and there was a war on'. But that's what a dog murderer would say.

To add insult to dog execution (it's a phrase, look it up), by November many people realised it wasn't all that necessary. *The Times* lamented that it had become clear they were being killed for no reason at all, other than the fact it was inconvenient to keep them alive. In fact, the pets that survived the killing frenzy would survive the rest of the war alive, healthy and un-euthanised.

Britain was obviously on the side of the goodies during the Second World War. But it must have made the other side's propagandists' jobs a lot easier to look over at the UK and see us murdering the shit out of nearly half a million floofies in week one before a bomb had even been dropped for no real reason whatsoever.

WE ABUSED SOME BLOKE FOR YEARS FOR ATTEMPTING TO STAY DRY

The idea of putting a bit of cloth above your head so that it gets wet before you do has been around for thousands of years. You'd think as an island nation that invaded half of the world just to get away from our own weather that we would have killed for a device that would let us stay dry without having to e.g. invade India and live there, but the umbrella caught on in Britain surprisingly late.

The British public genuinely regarded the idea of not getting soaked when it's pissing it down as 'too French', with accounts saying we called people a 'mincing Frenchman'[6] if they were caught using one. In fact, the first man who tried to start carrying an umbrella was mocked mercilessly and pelted with abuse and projectiles, and one man tried to run him down with a horse.

Jonas Hanway was a British man who just wanted to stay dry. In the early 1750s he started carrying an umbrella with him, and to the shock of everyone in London at the time, he actually used it, the absolute Frenchman. When he put it up, passers-by shouted, booed and jeered at him. There's no record of precise insults used against him, but it was probably along the lines of the Georgian equivalent of 'oh too good to contract pneumonia are you, you hoity-toity admittedly quite dry Parisian fucking weirdo?'

He especially came under attack from people who were terrified of umbrellas. Coach drivers hated him for it, because they (quite rightly) saw it as a threat to their business. When it rained, people used to rush to get in their coaches. If the umbrella caught on their whole business model of waiting for England's crap weather to be crap was fucked. They liked to think people enjoyed their company and service, but deep down they knew they were just a horse-drawn way to stay dry.

Sedan chair carriers also hated Umbrella Boy for the same reason. Why would anyone pay to have two slightly posh-looking men in top hats carry you around very slowly like a parcel, when what you really want to do was stand under a dry thing.

Cab drivers and coach drivers, normally rivals, united in their hatred of Jonas and regular-ly pelted him with rubbish, not fully comprehending that one of the many benefits of using an umbrella is it stops stuff from hitting you. A hansom cab driver* tried to run over Jonas with his coach. Jonas dodged the attack and in return gave the driver a 'thrashing' using his umbrella, thus demonstrating to any onlookers how versatile umbrellas truly are.

To complicate things a bit, Jonas was also a bellend. He was a big advocate for solitary con-finement and was against letting tea and Jewish people into the UK. Ergo, perhaps the abuse was justified – it just would have been nice if it had been about the racism rather than for using an object we went on to adore. We ended up using the umbrella so much, in fact, that it has become part of our national stereotype. If we had to shout abuse, and it would appear we did, we should have led with, 'Oi that umbrella looks both practical and suave, I quite fancy getting me one of those, you trendsetting but problematic antisemitic and tea-hating arsehole.'

*A hansom cab is a type of horse-drawn carriage. No record survives about how fuckable the driver was.

WE PASSED A LAW WHICH FORCED MOST OF THE COUNTRY TO WEAR A LITTLE BOBBLE HAT ON SUNDAYS

We've done a lot of weird shit to the poor in our time but forcing them to wear hats that they don't want to wear is up there with taxing them for growing beards (which it's also rumoured we did).

In 1571, the English Monmouth hat was going out of fashion. After enjoying a long era of being England's favourite woollen knitted headwear, all of a sudden it was *soooo* 1562. Nobody wanted to wear them any more. The hats that had once been the favourite of Lords and Earls were now the 16th-century equivalent of Crocs.

So what could be done about the decline of a hat that nobody wanted? If you're the kind of person who thinks the answer is, 'I guess let the hat die out then' – you have failed to understand the lengths the monarchy will protect garments over the rights of the poor. Queen Elizabeth I decided to force people to wear them by law. Nothing keeps an item in fashion like a Parliament decree to wear it against your will.

Generous as she was, she only forced this upon people who didn't have any money. In an act of Parliament, she stated that everyone except for 'maids, ladies, gentlewomen, noble personages, and every Lord, knight and gentleman of twenty marks land' should have to wear on Sundays a 'Cap of Wool knit, thicked and dressed in England, made within this Realm, and only dressed and finished by some of the Trade of Cappers, upon pain to forfeit for every Day of not wearing three Shillings four Pence'.[7] Since they were already poor, this could mean prison for non-payment.

Essentially, in the 16th century we had the literal fashion police, except they were forcing the poor to look shit on Sundays and making them poorer if they didn't comply. It's like if today's government decided that anyone under a certain bank balance should go out and buy assless chaps and start wearing them between 5 and 7 p.m. on pain of a fine.

The law kept the hat industry going for some years, although you'd hope at least some hatmakers felt it sucked the fun out of their job knowing that people only bought them because otherwise they might get thrown in the slammer with the paedos. It was repealed twenty-eight years later, not because it was a batshit idea to force people to wear hats on Sundays even during summer, but because they realised that enforcing people to wear a hat they didn't want to wear in their own homes was next to impossible. Who knew.

DARWIN ATE ENDANGERED SPECIES LIKE THEY WERE CORNISH PASTIES

When you imagine Charles Darwin, you probably picture a sensible grandpa-type, meticulously taking notes as he studied an exotic bird, nodding thoughtfully and saying 'hmm yes, this is definitely a science.'

But Darwin, famous evolutionist and naturalist, also went around chain-eating exotic species like they were goddamn flumps. He ate owls like they were chicken wings, and armadillos like they were the chocolate bar also called Armadillos. Once, after loading his ship up with them in the Galapagos, he and his crew ate endangered tortoises all on the way home. He only realised how significant they were to his theory of evolution when he got back to England and had a closer look at the shells, which they had been using as some sort of makeshift soup bowls.

This wasn't even a one-off. He was part of the 'glutton club', a group of foodies who specifically liked to dine on 'strange flesh', a term Hannibal Lecter would label 'a bit fucking creepy to be honest with you Charles.' After spending several months trying to catch an extremely rare lesser rhea bird, he sat down and unwittingly ate one during a Christmas meal. When he realised what it was, he jumped up in the middle of the meal and desperately tried to scrape what was left off his plate for his experiments, in what might be the most scientifically important doggie bag of all time.

To be fair to Darwin, he didn't just accidentally use incredibly endangered animals as snacks, he was also partial to messing around with critically vulnerable animals on purpose for a bit of a giggle. Whilst in the Galapagos, he wrote about yanking iguanas' tails to see how they'd react, poking birds with his gun, and riding around on giant tortoises like they were a horse. In between twatting rare animals and eating their delicious endangered corpses, he discovered evolution to keep himself busy in his down time.

IRISH FAMINE (PART 1):
WE HELPED KILL 1 MILLION OF OUR NEIGHBOURS BY APPLYING A THEORY ABOUT RABBITS TO THEM

In a long list of terrible things the British have done over the years, 'doing a famine on our next-door neighbours' is up there. The Great Famine (often referred to as the 'potato famine' in the UK as a way of implying a million fussy Irish people died because they wouldn't eat mash) began in 1845, when a fungus began to grow on Ireland's main source of food.

If they'd had access to other varieties of disease-free potato or other crops, the suffering that saw one million die might not have been quite as bad it was. But the British continued policies such as artificially inflating grain prices (through tariffs on imports from America), which made grain unaffordable to the poor in Ireland and kept farmers shipping out grain to the British. Classic.

Now all this sounds terrible, but it turns out the ideology behind it was also evil but more so. As well as a dose of good old fashioned anti-Catholicism, the people in charge of relief in Ireland were also motivated by a belief that a theory based on rabbits applied to the Irish.

Thomas Malthus, a cleric and scholar, had a popular-ish theory that, whilst food supplies increased steadily, populations grew exponentially – to a point that they could no longer be sustained by the food supplies. At this point, he thought populations would 'correct' themselves through starvation and disease*. Intervening and trying to save people – e.g. by giving starving people food – would only prolong suffering, and should be avoided in favour of letting them die out until the population reached a sustainable level.

This was all well and good in theory (it wasn't though), but unfortunately people in power saw the famine in Ireland and thought 'that's happening in practice, that is. Sod it, let's give this a try.' Sir Charles Trevelyan, colonial administrator in charge of famine relief to Ireland, took Malthus's theory of 'just let them die' and applied it to the country he was in charge of specifically keeping alive and well.

Armed with this philosophy and too much power over laws, over the next few years Trevelyan basically became Thanos from the *Avengers* films but with corn tariffs instead of a fancy glove.

This throbber will return in part 2 of the Irish Famine.

and there's no way he didn't say this sitting in a lair within a volcano whilst stroking a cat before cackling.

WE CLEANED CHIMNEYS BY LOBBING A GOOSE UP THE FLUE IN A CREATIVE TAX-AVOIDANCE EFFORT

Picture a chimney sweep. Now picture Dick Van Dyke (don't lie, you pictured Dick Van Dyke the first time) strapping a goose's feet together and throwing it down the chimney during the second verse of 'Chim Chim Cher-ee' whilst Mary Poppins stands there letting the whole thing happen like it's a perfectly normal thing to do.

The life of a chimney sweep was not pleasant. During the 17th and 18th centuries, tax was paid on the size of the house, which was determined by the number of chimneys that house had. Keen to avoid tax, richer households would connect fireplaces together to the main chimney using smaller and smaller flues. They became so tiny that the only way to get them clean was to ram a child up them, which everyone knows wealthier Victorians did with reckless abandon.

Kids as young as seven were fired up chimneys to sweep them, enduring terrible conditions. The contact with the soot gave them a 'chimney sweeps' carcinoma'* primarily affecting the testicles, because the chimney was so hot and sweaty that the soot would make its way down to the scrotal sack, causing chronic irritation leading to the condition.

At home too, conditions were terrible and children were often made to sleep under sacks of soot in basements with several other chimney sweeps – probably why they were known to get a bit sleepy up the chimneys. Fortunately masters were kind and gave them a few minutes' leeway before setting a fire to try and burn them out. Weirdly, at first the chimney sweeps weren't even paid, and would only earn money by selling the soot as fertiliser. So when house owners tapped their watches and muttered, 'that small child is taking the piss here, guess I'll burn him out', they weren't even paying him for the privilege.

So more humane methods were created – at least for humans. Chimney sweeps would grab a goose, tie its feet together (though in some accounts it would be tied by the neck for horror factor) and then throw it down the chimney. It would freak the fuck out and start flapping around, knocking all the soot off the walls in a desperate attempt either to fly or alert the RSPB.

It spawned the phrase 'the blacker the goose the cleaner the flue' whereas in any civilised society it would have led to the saying, 'what in the name of fuck are you doing with that goose, Craig? No. Bad Craig.'

Quick tip: It's never a great sign on career day when they mention an occupation has its own type of cancer named after it.

WE USED TO DELIBERATELY TRY TO MAKE PEOPLE CRY ON VALENTINE'S DAY

Valentine's Day is a day when people around the world celebrate love. We used to use it as a day to tell strangers we thought they were wankers.

In Victorian Britain, as well as regular 'you're alright' Valentine's cards, a tradition started where people sent out 'Vinegar Valentines' – cards to tell strangers, or even friends, that you secretly hated them, or some other horrible thing that you would never say to their face.

In what was essentially the Beta version of the Internet, people would send out cards designed to insult the recipient, focusing on everything from how fugly they were, to highlighting a massive personality defect that made them fundamentally unlovable. They would inform the reader, through a crudely drawn cartoon and a poem, that they were preachy, shrews, stingy or even an alcoholic, even though a 'here's a caricature of what you look like, you big drunk' card from Clintons probably isn't the most tactful way of staging an intervention.

'BALD HEAD' one read in all caps, underneath a picture of a man with an undeniably big bald head.

'Your bright shining pate is seen at all shows,
and invariably down in the bald-headed rows,
where you make conspicuous by your tender care,
your true ardent love for that one lonesome hair.'[8]

Imagine being alone on Valentine's day, receiving a card, paying the postage (the sender would deliberately not pay it so that you had to purchase your own insult), opening it up and finding out 'ah I'm being informed I'm bald' as if you'd never encountered a mirror.

So popular were Vinegar Valentines, that they specialised as much as birthday cards. There were cards made to insult just about anyone in any profession, empowering the buyer to get as specific and personal as they liked.

There were even reports of cards sent out encouraging people to commit suicide, and other reports that someone did commit suicide after receiving one. You think card shops are bad now – imagine the crush of people emerging from their basements in early February to make someone who once rejected them feel a bit sad on Valentine's Day.

'I want to insult a doctor.'

'Try the doctor section.'

'Need to call him a big baldy twat.'

'Big baldy twat doctor section, aisle three.'

'Hmm, it's good but I really want him to kill himself.'

'Kill yourself you big baldy twat, aisle three.'

'He's forty-seven and called Greg.'

'Sir, you can keep listing very specific requirements and I'm going to keep telling you it's in aisle three.'

WE MADE WOMEN WEAR MUZZLES

The majority of entries in this book are about the English being bellends. Well, take a short break from being called a bellend, English folks, because some time before 1567 in Scotland we invented muzzles for women.

The scold's bridle was a metal contraption or sometimes a weird-looking mask that went over the head, with another piece of metal that slid into the mouth of the wearer and either compressed the tongue or raised it, resulting in excessive salivation and mouth fatigue. To give you an idea of the level of respect that existed for these women who were made to wear the mask, this idea was directly taken from how we treat a horse. A bridle is usually placed on a horse's mouth as a way of leading it around, and reins were fitted to the side of the human mask too for the same purpose.

You'd think that women would have to have done something pretty awful to get placed in one of these horrible contraptions, something so unspeakable that, though nobody likes corporal punishment any more, would at least make you go 'ok yeah fair play, I personally wouldn't go that far but I get why a severe punishment was needed.' But no. Women would be placed in these torture masks for the crimes of being a bit rude, 'nagging', gossiping, or doing a wrong kind of religion in public.

Once in the muzzle, they'd be led through town by their horse reins, or left in a public place for everyone to see as they salivated and tried not to move their mouth. Some of the contraptions had a spike on the mouthpiece, meaning that if you moved your tongue you'd impale it, making speaking, eating or waggling your tongue about to fight off the boredom impossible without bleeding profusely.

Though mainly ordered by courts, they were also used by husbands as a way of humiliating their wives. Some women were even made to wear the masks for speaking out about mistreatment from their husbands. Which is a vicious cycle to get into as their husbands clearly were the kind of sadistic bastards who would muzzle their wives at the slightest sign that they would tell anybody about how sadistic and bastardy they were.

The use of the scold's bridle continued in this way till as late as 1856, even though it should have ended the very first time this conversation happened:

'Why have you got your wife in that muzzle, Kenneth?'

'She said I'd been mistreating her.'

'I don't want to be rude, Kenneth, as you strike me as a dangerous fucking psychopath, but you are sort of leading her about town in a horse muzzle so maybe she's got a point?'

WE HATCHED A PLAN TO WIPE OUT A NATION'S FOOD SUPPLY USING DELICIOUS ANTHRAX CAKE

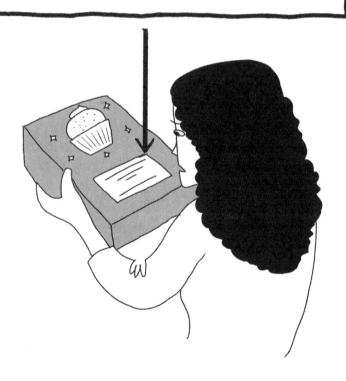

In 1942, under instruction from Winston Churchill, British scientists hatched a plan to kill Germany's cows by feeding them anthrax. Nuclear weapons weren't ready yet and we needed a way of forcing the Germans to surrender as quickly as possible, so we settled on caking them to death in an initiative named Project Vegetarian.

The idea was to bake a load of biologically weaponised cattle cakes (cakes made from linseed and ram-packed full of anthrax instead of icing) and drop them over agricultural areas of Germany. Then, unsuspecting and innocent cows would rush towards the treats thinking they're about to get a Linzertorte (they're German, if they're aware of the concept of cakes they aren't thinking Eccles) and instead get a tasty mouthful of anthrax. These cows would then get infected, infect humans, and die, causing mass famine and anthrax contamination in Germany and Europe that would take decades to recover from. If all went right with the plan, millions of people could die over many years of misery. It was sort of like the *Great British Bake Off*, but instead of a nice picnic where all the contestants return, it ends with mass murder.

At this stage I'd like to point out that the cows had not picked a side. None of these cows were even the remotest bit Hitlery. They went about their days eating grass in a politically neutral way, like a bovine version of Switzerland. If you had to ascertain what side they were on, in fact, they spent a lot of their time enthusiastically shitting on Nazi fields, so an argument could be made that we were about to declare biological warfare on the animal regiment of our own resistance.

Because we're a thorough bunch of bastards, we tested out the idea first. In late 1942 we took control of Gruinard Island, a tiny private island off the coast of Scotland, in order to murder some sheep. A flock was shipped over, and we detonated a bomb inside a big ball of anthrax cakes nearby. The strain we tested on the island was particularly virulent, and within days the entire flock was dead. We looked around the piles of innocent sheep corpses and declared another job well done.

Unfortunately, it was *too* effective. The whole island became contaminated with anthrax and had to be quarantined immediately so that we didn't anthrax ourselves. The sheep were buried to try and stop the spread, but one sheep ended up floating its way across the sea to mainland Scotland where a dog ate it. The dog then passed this onto other pets, and before we knew it, over a hundred pets were dead. Although, I guess, you could also chalk it up as a win by arguing they were Nazi pets as they had spent a lot of time shitting on Britain's pavements.

The island remained infected for the next fifty years before we dealt with the problem. Luckily we learned our lesson and filed the plans under 'what the fuck were we thinking' and scrapped them. I am, of course, taking the piss. In 1943 and 1944, we cooked up five million anthrax cakes and created customised RAF planes to drop them. We didn't do it only because it looked like Germany was close to surrendering, and we knew that the mess would take decades to clear up.

WE BUILT A THOUSAND-MILE HEDGE THROUGH INDIA TO MAKE SALT A TAD MORE EXPENSIVE

One of the few pleasures of following politics in modern Britain is saying, 'Well at least we aren't as bad as Trump, that guy has lost it.' Especially when he brings up his border wall, thinking that nobody in Mexico has heard of ladders or planes.

But in our past we did something of equal insanity, if a tad more Alan Titchmarshy. To add insult to injury, the reasons behind our wall were really twattish. Trump, in his own ridiculous, racist and ignorant way, at least thinks that his wall is helping to protect the country. We built ours to make salt slightly more profitable.

Smugglers had been smuggling (as is their duty) salt across India due to the ridiculously high tax the British charged on it. So, naturally, we lowered tax to a reasonable level spent thirty years building a 1,000 mile hedge across the Inland Customs Line, a barrier which the British used to enforce the Salt Tax stopping smugglers getting through.

First, we half-arsed it, piling up bits of dead tree. This failed when we had to replace it every year. Some clever border guards caught on to this and started planting live trees and hedges instead. But due to the arid landscape, which was also prone to flooding, and the surprisingly little training that the British army dedicated to horticulture at the time, this was more difficult than they expected. Trees withered and died in some places, and were swept away by floods in others.

When we finally did get trees and hedges to grow, we had a further problem when a plague of rats moved into one section of the hedge. The guards brought in feral cats to deal with the rat problem, like a cartoon villain or someone in a nursery rhyme would, and soon anyone who wanted to smuggle salt through the hedge would have to explain why that salt was covered in the blood of rats and poo of cats to their buyers.

Overall we spent around three decades fighting rats and training guards to be guard-iners, until finally the hedge was finished. W.S. Halsey, Commissioner of Inland Customs, visited the hedge and found it was, in parts, 12 feet tall and 14 feet deep. By 1878, it was 1,100 miles long and was policed by 12,000 guards tasked to keep salt – which famously isn't even heroin, guns or crack – from crossing the border.

The British stopped funding the project that same year, realising it to be bat as well as rat and cat shit crazy.

WE SAVED BILLIONS OF LIVES IN A BELLENDY WAY

Famed Brit Edward Jenner eradicated a disease that was killing fifty million people a year. He saved an impossible number of lives, possibly even going into billions. He may have saved more lives than any other human in history. But you can't make an omelette without breaking eggs. And by eggs I mean eight-year-old kids.

In 1796, smallpox was running rampant. It killed around 10 percent of the population, and up to 20 percent of people dumb enough to live in the city, where to repeat the last bit of this sentence, 20 percent of the population was being killed by an infectious disease.

Jenner was a physician who would deliberately infect children with small amounts of smallpox in order to inoculate them. Many of them of course died, but this was standard practice and was preferable to them receiving a larger dose of smallpox later on. Don't judge the wanker just yet.

Living in a rural area, Jenner had heard rumours that milkmaids were immune to smallpox. He guessed, based on theirs and others' reports, that their immunity came from being exposed to cowpox, which was similar to smallpox. He decided to test this hypothesis by injecting the pus of an infected milkmaid into the eight-year-old son of his gardener. (You can start judging now.)

There are some grey areas when it comes to medical research, but cutting your employee's son and rubbing a deadly disease into the wound is what's scientifically known as 'a bit of a no-no'. Imagine if your own boss came to you and asked:

'Hey, do you mind if I borrow your son?'

'Why?'

'You'll get him back. Probably. One way or the other.'

'Do you mind if I just have a quick chat with HR?'

'Look just let me inject the fucking plague into your son, do you want to remain employed yes or no?'

One might say there's quite a lot of coercion involved.

And so Jenner injected the pus from cowpox-infected milkmaid Sarah Nelmes into eight-year-old James Phipps. Phipps got ill, the predictable little shit, and took ten days to recover. Having successfully not killed a boy, Jenner pushed his luck again and injected him with actual smallpox this time.

It was a huge risk. If he got it wrong, who would mow his lawn? You can't exactly tell the father of the kid you killed 'I think you missed a bit whilst strimming' but you also can't fire the father of the kid you just killed without looking like a dick. Phipps shared his bed with two siblings as well, risking wiping out a whole generation of gardeners in one go. However, it paid off. Phipps was immune. Jenner injected the boy, who wasn't being compensated for his trouble, a further twenty times just to be sure.

When he tried to publish his paper, it was rejected, leading Jenner to continue to experiment on poor farm workers, their children and workhouse inmates over the next two years. Basically, if they were vulnerable, Jenner was waiting nearby in the shadows ready to pounce with a syringe full of deadly disease. His experiments were successful, and he went on to save a ridiculous number of lives through his willingness to inject the poor based on scant and mainly anecdotal evidence. Superhero? Sure. Bellend? Absolutely.

WE SHIPPED PEOPLE TO THE OTHER SIDE OF THE PLANET FOR RECEIVING STOLEN BACON

In 1776, the USA became independent. This gave us a problem in that America used to be where we dumped a lot of our criminals. The problem was compounded by the growing number of people turning to crime, due to population growth, overcrowding, unemployment and poverty.

Fortunately, in 1770, James Cook had claimed the east coast of Australia for the British.* We saw a beautiful sprawling paradise thousands of miles away and thought 'what a lovely place to dispose of the poor we can't afford to throw in the clink'.

In the first shipment of our convicts to Australia in 1788, we sent 775 prisoners on 11 ships including one vessel named – I shit you not – *Friendship*. The convicts were chained below decks for the six months of their gruelling voyage. About 10 per cent died on that first journey and around 30 per cent on later trips. The first shipment of criminals was sent with only enough food to last until they'd established their own food supplies. Unfortunately, not enough skilled farmers committed crimes that year, and so the people who arrived lacked the expertise to farm enough food to live, and deaths due to food shortages were high. Deportation was basically like the death penalty but with a fun roulette element.

Once the colonies were survivable, the horror was far from over. Before you could say 'surf's up' the people who survived the journey were set to back-breaking work creating colonies. Work in the penal colonies was hard, and punishments were notoriously brutal. People convicted of further crimes whilst in the penal colonies could be sent to Norfolk Island, a penal colony between Australia and New Zealand, where they'd face even worse conditions. On this island punishments included lashing people sometimes nearly 100 times in one sitting. After one mutiny at the Norfolk Island prison in 1834, a vicar visited to inform the prisoners who was to be executed. To give you an indication of the conditions he found at the prison, he wrote 'it is a literal fact that each man who heard his reprieve wept bitterly, and that each man who heard of his condemnation to death went down on his knees with dry eyes, and thanked God,'[9] making Norfolk Island only mildly worse than the UK's original Norfolk.

So what kind of horrendous crimes would you have to commit to get yourself sent across the world to such harsh conditions and treatment? Anything from stealing a single handkerchief to impersonating a naval officer.

People convicted of serious crimes (murder, rape etc.) were executed. Deportation to penal colonies was mainly reserved for petty criminals, who we believed couldn't be reformed but needed to be kept out of society. We're talking really, really petty crime. One of the captives on the earlier fleets of ships, for instance, was a seventy-year-old woman who had been caught stealing cheese to eat. She got shipped to the furthest point on the planet from us during her old age because of a crime mainly committed by cartoon mice. Another aboard the first fleet – and so clearly one of our top priorities for urgently getting kicked out of the country – was Jane Castings, a twenty-year-old convicted of receiving stolen bacon. Between 1788 and 1868 we sent over 160,000 convicts over to the penal colonies in Australia, mostly for similarly small crimes (such as larceny of a hat) or for rebelling against British rule in Ireland. Ah, justice.

If you're asking 'but what about the people who already inhabited Australia' you have not been paying attention to how much of a shit we give about people who live in countries that aren't us. We're basically like the toddlers of the world, waddling about the place and saying, 'THIS IS MINE' when we find things we want.

Nerve agents are grim. They attach to enzymes between your nerve cells and muscles, causing a build-up of acetylcholine (a natural neurotransmitter in your body) which makes your muscles go haywire. Before you know it, you are in respiratory failure, losing consciousness whilst convulsing, going into paralysis and excessively drooling, all whilst experiencing the worst diarrhoea of your life.

Which is why you don't want to, for instance, subject 3,100 of your own military personnel to it on purpose over the course of forty years, which is precisely what we did.

During the last few years of the Second World War, the Nazis began developing nerve gas. Not letting a fortnight go by before copying the heinous and grotesque weapons from the deranged imaginations of the baddies, Britain began testing nerve gas on our own military in the hope of manufacturing massive quantities of it ourselves.

The experiments, carried out at a military defence lab at Porton Down, saw thousands of servicemen – some of whom say they had been told they were getting cold medicine – subjected to the nerve agent sarin.

During one phase of the experiments, the military wanted to answer the completely non-sinister Good Guy question of 'how much nerve gas would it take to kill a man through clothes or on the skin'. To estimate this, they got groups of five volunteers. They proceeded to tape a piece of cloth to one of their arms each, and ask them to step into a gas chamber, wearing no protective clothing but a respirator and, for some reason, a woollen hat. They'd then drop sarin onto the volunteer's cloth patch, and measure the reaction in their blood.

During one test, a man named Kelly slipped into a coma. In response to this, the military lowered the doses for everyone else slightly, from 300 mg of deadly nerve agent to 200 mg of a still incredibly deadly nerve agent.

This lower dose was given to twenty-year-old Leading Aircraftman Ronald George Maddison on 6 May 1953. He had been offered 15 shillings (which he was going to use to buy an engagement ring for his girlfriend Mary) and three days of leave to take part in the experiment. Like thousands of others – and the four other volunteers in the gas chamber with him – Ronald was given his dose, but after twenty minutes he reported not feeling well, and collapsed. He was taken away and treated, but ultimately died forty-five minutes later.

In separate experiments at Porton Down, servicemen had been told they were getting cold medicine before being given a big hit of LSD, leading to terrifying hallucinations. Ronald's family say that he too believed he was being given cold medicine during the experiment, before he was killed by sarin.

Ronald's family were at first sworn to secrecy under the Official Secrets Act, and were given his body in a steel coffin, bolted so that nobody could look inside. Which is always a sign that everything is above board. For good measure, the military also kept a lot of Ronald's organs, including parts of his skin, muscles spinal cord tissue, gut, lung and brain.

They didn't tell Ronald's family this because they had also sworn themselves to secrecy.

WE USED A CRAP PLOT AS AN EXCUSE TO PURSUE OUR FAVOURITE ACTIVITY OF MURDERING PEOPLE ON RELIGIOUS GROUNDS

For many years of our history, we were pretty fickle about which religion we were persecuting. Then in 1553, Mary I, a Catholic, took to the throne and started burning people who had been forced to become Protestants by her dad and her brother. After she executed 283 people, mostly by burning them at the stake, and persuaded a lot of Protestants that maybe Catholicism was the way to go after all, Queen Elizabeth I took to the throne and started persecuting Catholics again. Elizabeth introduced new laws that barred Catholics from civil office and later from studying at universities. As well as that, if you didn't fancy attending an Anglican church you'd better have been loaded because you would get a massive fine. And if you enjoyed Catholic mass you'd also better enjoy being thrown in the slammer, because that was the new penalty for attending it.

Later on, the laws were strengthened and priests were kicked out of the country, under threat of execution if they didn't leave. Priest Edmund Campion, when sentenced to death, made the point that he was being executed for being a priest of the church that until recently was followed by everyone in England, and so in a way they were condemning their own ancestors. This would have got a few retweets in modern times, but the judge ordered him to be dragged through the streets by a horse, hung but taken down whilst still alive, and then have his genitals cut off and his entrails taken out and burned in front of him. So, you know. We weren't great to Catholics.

King James I strengthened this legislation which was already a touch too 'KILL ALL CATHO-LICS' for comfort, and a group of them decided to respond with some barbaric actions of their own. Led and masterminded by Robert Catesby, the gunpowder plotters decided to blow up the House of Lords and the King with it. As cool as it sounds, it wasn't the best put together plot imaginable. At one point, Rob's servant accidentally learned of the plot and had to be brought into the conspiracy in case he blabbed. It's like if one of Osama Bin Laden's inner circle was there only because he found the plans whilst having a bit of a tidy. Catesby was also a known traitor – yet he rented an undercroft underneath the Houses of Parliament in his own name, which is at best a bit of a tactical whoopsie. When their plot was uncovered after someone, likely one of the conspirators, sent a letter to the government warning of the plot, it was Guy Fawkes who was caught. He gave his name as 'John Johnson' which is only slightly better as an alias than 'Mr Innocent McMadeupname'. It doesn't exactly scream 'these group of evil geniuses have really planned ahead'.

The plot was so bad that some highly disputed historians (and conspiracy theorists at the time) have suggested the government must have known about it, and let it continue for as long as possible so that they could use it as a reason to crack down on Catholics (again).

After the plot was foiled and everyone had been tortured, then dispatched in the most horrible ways imaginable, the British used the terrorist plot as an excuse to crack down on a religious minority, rather than just terrorists – a habit we still haven't really grown out of.

As an extra 'fuck you', we then decided to celebrate the burning of Guy Fawkes for hundreds of years. And he wasn't even the man who came up with the plot, just the expendable guy who got told to take on the task of lighting the fuse. It would be like if history books today ignored the role of Hitler and saved the blame for Hitler's pool boy.

WE TURNED WOMEN MURDER INTO A REAL MONEY-MAKER

The Salem Witch Trials in America were as dumb as they were brutal. And they were really, really dumb. But the witch trials in Britain were far worse, on a bigger scale, and even turned the systematic murder of innocent women into a profitable business model.

In the 1640s, British people were really getting into the hot new craze of accusing each other of being witches then watching the trials and ensuing death. Executing witches had been around for a while as a niche, like Pokémon, but suddenly saw a resurgence towards the mid-17th century and now everyone was doing it, like the later released Pokémon Go.*

Enter Matthew Hopkins. If there's one sure fire way of identifying a psychopath, you can't go far wrong with 'he's murdered so many women he's got his own murderer nom-de-plume', but nobody seems to have told people in the 1600s that. This led to a situation where Matthew, a man who called himself 'The Witch-finder General', was allowed to go around killing women like they were characters in *Game of Thrones*.

Matthew looked on at the cacophony of superstition, misogyny and human suffering and thought 'yeah I reckon I could make a few quid out of this'. So he travelled to towns in the East of England offering his services as a finder of witches, the first of several witch-killing businessmen to do so. For vast sums of cash he would go into a town, root out 'witches' and have them executed. In Ipswich his costs were so high they had to introduce a special local tax rate in order to pay for his women-killing services.

Matthew was good at getting confessions. Unsanctioned torture was illegal at the time**, but he got around this by rebranding obvious torture as an 'interrogation'. One of his favourite early methods was sleep deprivation. The first person he tortured was eighty-year-old widow and amputee Elizabeth Clarke, who was accused by a local tailor of being a witch. Hopkins kept the elderly lady awake for four days and nights, making her get up and walk around the house on her one leg if it looked like she might want a snooze, as people are generally known to do at least three times a day in their eighties.

Eventually she gave in and confessed, telling Hopkins that she 'had carnal copulation with the devil for six or seven years' – which would be quite impressive physically speaking even if you weren't so old that you 'like that handsome young Nigel Farage chap' and think that *Mrs Brown's Boys* is acceptable television.

But one confession of being Satan's fuckbuddy wasn't good enough for Matthew, and he pushed her further until she also accused some random other women in the town, in a blatant attempt to get some repeat business. It's a miracle he didn't get tried as a witch himself, considering every time he saw a vulnerable woman he could potentially murder, his eyes would spin round and form dollar signs like he was in a cartoon.

Elizabeth was hanged on her own confession, as well as Matthew's compelling evidence that he had seen one of her 'evil helpers', a small and perfectly ordinary baby he claimed was involved in her witchcraft. Now having a taste for the torture of women and a hundred per cent success rate, he moved around the country selling his services, like if Charles Manson had monetised himself and started selling his murder services door to door.

Over the next two years he was responsible for the deaths of around 300 people, most of whom were women and zero of whom had actual magical powers.

For legal purposes I should explain Pokémon revolves around the murder of cute animals, not human women.
**King James VI of Scotland and I of England was also torturing 'witches' around the same time, so it wasn't that illegal.*

WE STOLE AN ISLAND FROM ITS RIGHTFUL OWNERS BY PRETENDING THEY DIDN'T EXIST

When the British Empire was breaking up, we couldn't resist one last act of being a total arsehole just for old times' sake.

That opportunity came when it was time to give back Mauritius and grant it independence. America, however, had their eye on Diego Garcia, part of the Chagos Islands (which were about to fall under Mauritian sovereignty) – they wanted it as a military base in order to monitor Soviet activity. Ergo, a sordid deal was struck with the British. In return for leasing the Chagos Islands, Britain would get a major contribution to our Polaris submarine programme and one of those American hair ruffles we love so much. Through pressure on Mauritius, which they would later say amounted to forcing them to do it, we were able to keep this uninhabited island in the middle of the ocean as ours, perfect for use as a military base.

Unfortunately, there was a problem, in that the island actually *was* inhabited. By around 1,800 people, in fact, mainly descendants of slaves. If the UN found out about them, they would need to be recognised as people 'whose democratic rights have to be safeguarded'. The UK had a solution though, and brace yourselves because it's a fucking doozy: we would simply pretend to the world that they weren't really there at all. We reclassified the population, many of whom had been there for five generations, as 'temporary workers' on the island, belonging elsewhere and with no right to residence.

Americans moved onto the island and began building a base right away. Whenever an islander received urgent medical treatment away from the island in Mauritius, they were not allowed back in. If someone else went to then check their recently hospitalised and now exiled relative was ok, they too would find themselves unable to return home. If you booked a holiday, you'd sure as hell hope you picked somewhere you'd like to live permanently, because buddy, we were not letting you back in.

In one final act of intimidation, Sir Bruce Greatbatch, governor of the Seychelles and man in charge of 'sanitising'* the island, ordered all the dogs of the island to be rounded up and gassed in front of their owners. Almost 1,000 pets were caught and put to death using the exhaust fumes from American military vehicles on the island, which, and I know it's not the main thing, isn't even very eco-friendly.

The intimidation worked. When someone starts gassing your dogs to death at the same time as *pretending to the world that you don't live there at all and there are no records of you*, you tend to get the message. At least you don't hang around to find out if it was just a mass dog death-based wacky misunderstanding.

The remaining population, like a person at a dinner party who has just noticed the host has been yawning and glancing at their watch for the past hour and also nodding pointedly at a gun, took the hint and left on ships provided by their 'hosts'. They were allowed only one suitcase each. After briefly stopping in the Seychelles, where they were kept in a prison, they were then transported to Mauritius, where they were unceremoniously told to get out.

The military base went on to be used as a place where the CIA detained people unlawfully, allegedly to torture them, and we later took off from the base to bomb Iraq. To this day, we have only given minimal compensation to the families we booted out, and have not given the island back.

*No goody has ever been told to sanitise anything. If your job is to sanitise something and it's not some kind of toilet, congratulations: you are on the side of the baddies.

WE BANNED CHRISTMAS, THEN MURDERED IT

It's hard to say the words 'they banned Christmas' without sounding like I'm sat here wearing a St George's Cross flag and smashing up Easter Eggs with a can of Special Brew just in case they're halal, but we did actually ban Christmas in England for thirteen years.

Oliver Cromwell had fought a long and brutal civil war which split the country. During the first part of the war his band of Roundheads had done horrible things. During the second, they did some more. For example, they held a siege of the town of Colchester that lasted so long civilians had to eat dog as well as their candles. This is only marginally made better by the fact that candles were made of mutton wax. It's still dog with a side of candle, though, which is by no means laying on a feast. And Colchester was a town that had broadly supported Oliver's own side. To put it mildly, he badly needed a PR win to keep people on board.

So in 1647 his Puritan movement actually sat down and used their power to ban Christmas, in a dick move that would stay in place right up until 1660. The Puritans felt that Christmas had become too immoral, fun and a festival of 'carnal and sensual delights' which is basically just listing the good bits of Christmas in a slightly judgemental tone.

Festival days, including Christmas, were ordered to not be celebrated even with family, but instead to be spent in respectful contemplation, which isn't very Christmassy. Shops were forced to remain open (not just the traditional Tesco Express), decorations banned, and all nativities and feasts abolished. Instead, it was to be replaced with a day of fast. Which, I'm sure you'll agree, is a shit swap for a fuckload of cheese, pressies and whatever the 17th-century equivalent of *Die Hard* was.

In order to ensure people weren't just having a quiet one, guards would patrol the streets of London around Christmas confiscating any food that looked like it might be for a feast, snatching away any suspiciously plump-looking geese being carried around by Tiny Tim types.

People weren't even allowed to attend church, and in 1647 a bunch of church ministers were rounded up and jailed for attempting to celebrate Christmas in this way. On Christmas Day. Jailing senior members of the church for celebrating Christmas is pretty much the least Christmassy thing on record, other than the time Charles Dickens novelised *The Muppet Christmas Carol* and systematically removed all the muppets including Rizzo.

You won't be surprised to learn that the banning of fun did not go down well with people who enjoy fun. Christmassy riots broke out. In London, crowds assembled at Cornhill and put up Christmas decorations. The mayor was forced by law to dispatch guards to take down the decorations. The crowd resisted, and so began a Christmas Day twatting, as a group of soldiers were called in to break up the crowd before they did something really bad like sing 'Jingle Bells' or 'Away in a Fucking Manger'.

In Ipswich another riot broke out, in which a protestor got killed on Christmas Day. It later transpired that his name was also Christmas. And so it was that we the British killed Christmas on Christmas for trying to celebrate Christmas. Even the Grinch drew the line at homicide.

WE LET A COMPANY DEDICATED TO EVIL RUN MOST OF A CONTINENT

In 1600 a company, led by Sir Thomas Smythe, formally asked for Queen Elizabeth I's permission to begin trading with the eastern hemisphere. As a lot of other countries were already helping themselves to Asia, the British East India Company were quite late to the game, but what they lacked in timing they more than made up for in ruthlessness and/or not really giving a shit about exploiting everybody (including slaves) to make money. They called themselves at times the 'Honourable' East India Company, which is a massive red flag. It's like how North Korea calls themselves the Democratic Republic of North Korea, or if some guy late at night at a bus shelter introduces himself as 'Not Even Remotely Stabby Ben'.

At first the company traded in silk, salt and spices, but the company, like an out-of-control branch of WHSmith, soon strayed from its company mission statement and started diversifying into:

Slavery
They were involved in the East Africa slave trade as well as transporting slaves from the west coast of Africa to settlements in India and Asia.

King bribery
They awarded King Charles II annual gifts of massive sacks of money and massive loans for war. The relationship went two ways. In the 1670s King Charles II gave the East India Company powers to acquire territory and troops, as well as make war and even mint money.

Stealing regions
Not satisfied with mere trading of people as well as spice, the company, led by board member Josiah Child, decided to move into being a 'formidable martial government in India', and began assaults on Indian territories. Because they were allowed to have their own soldiers (an army of 260,000 men, more than twice the size of the actual British army at the time), the company was soon in control of a vast region.

Exploitation
When the company remembered it was still in the textiles business so it might have to sell a few clothes, it began exploiting the workforce in India using its army as an implied 'we can kill you if you don't make that dress pretty enough' threat. In Bengal, weavers under the 'employment' of the company were basically slaves. The company used fines, prison and flogging as a way to keep them 'motivated'. Many desperate weavers reportedly chopped off their own thumbs to escape the work.

Just straight up stealing stuff
Pretence that the company wasn't just a big front for crime began to drop, as they carried out sanctioned looting. One senior official of the Mughal regime recorded that 'Indians were tortured to disclose their treasure; cities, towns and villages ransacked; *jaghires* and provinces purloined: these were the "delights" and "religions" of the directors and their servants.'[10]

The company we allowed to rule whole countries were not, it was fair to say, Fair Trade.

RICHARD THE LIONHEART, ENGLISH LEGEND, HATED ENGLAND AND THE ENGLISH

Everyone knows Richard the Lionheart, the brave warrior King of England, who fought in the Third Crusades and, let's be honest here, shows up at the end of all the Robin Hood films to signify King John's reign is over and everything is somehow fine now. Sometimes Robin Hood is a human, sometimes he's some sort of fox. Richard the Lionheart – class act that he is – barely bats an eyelid when confronted with a grotesque talking fox that's somehow learned to wear people clothes, so focused is he on his job of being a great King.

Richard has somehow become a good guy figure in English history even though he:

Hated England
Richard didn't like hanging around in England very much, and spent most of his life abroad. Despite being born in England and loved by the English, one of our best-loved legends was basically French. His dad (Henry II of England) was French, his mother Eleanor of Aquitaine was French. He spoke little English, hated the weather and the culture, and visited England only twice as an adult.

Was a terrible King
He basically saw being King as a way to fund going around Europe and the Middle East fighting wars and pillaging towns. He did this for nine-and-a-half years, out of his ten years as king. He must be laughing in his grave that we all remember King John for being crap at a job he completely eschewed.

Disembowelled thousands of hostages
I may have buried the lede here. In late August 1191, as part of the Third Crusade, Richard conquered the city of Acre and took 2–3,000 Muslims as hostages. Richard wanted to exchange the prisoners for the True Cross (supposedly the cross that Jesus was crucified on) from Saladin as well as 100,000 gold pieces and 1,600 Christian hostages. When the cross didn't show up quickly enough, Richard had all the prisoners (including many women and children) taken to the top of a hill where they were disembowelled and beheaded in full view of Saladin and his troops.

Flogged people for showing up to his coronation with gifts
On September 3 1189, Richard was crowned King of England in Westminster Abbey. Jewish people were barred from the ceremony. Despite this, some did show up, even bringing gifts for a King who wouldn't let them in. For their trouble, they were stripped, flogged and banished from the court.

A rumour spread around the city that Richard hated Jewish people and had wanted them killed, and so the people of London started attacking Jewish people, burning their homes and splashing holy water on them, baptising them against their will. Eventually it got out of hand and Richard issued instructions that Jewish people no longer be harmed. But the instructions were only very loosely enforced, and it wasn't long before another massacre took place in York.

Committed rape and murder
You won't be shocked to learn that the guy who ordered slaughters of thousands of men was also rumoured to have committed rapes and to have murdered his own subjects. You can see why he's limited to a very short cameo in the Disney version of Robin Hood.

WE BURNED A NATIVE AMERICAN VILLAGE TO THE GROUND BECAUSE WE SUSPECTED THEM OF STEALING A CUP

In 1585, Sir Richard Grenville headed an expedition to establish a permanent colony in what is now North Carolina. Richard and the crew landed on Roanoke Island, where they were guided by Manteo, the chief of a local tribe (who had made the mistake of befriending the English and travelling with us to England on several occasions, making him far less suspicious of the cunts who would one day go on to kill his mother).

Richard and a group of colonists were shown around by Manteo. They came to a friendly village, full of peaceful villagers who belonged to the Aquascogoc tribe. The villagers and colonists watched each other with interest, as the colonists were prepared a feast of soft-shell crab, soups, berries, beans and cornbread.

After several days of being entertained and fed, Grenville returned to his ship. There he found that the worst had happened. It's not clear how he figured it out, whether he always counted his crockery during the night just in case, but at some point, Grenville discovered that a cup was missing. Realising that his crew had been hosted and fed well, and the Aquascogoc may have seen it as a trade, or that maybe he'd dropped the cup somewhere so screw it, Grenville decided to let it slide.

I'm just kidding. Grenville headed back to the village, fully prepared to burn it to the fucking ground.

Grenville's men met the villagers on the shore and demanded the cup back, with no evidence that it hadn't just been misplaced. The villagers promised to return the cup, but by sunset the colonists remained cupless (apart from all the countless other cups in their possession).

So in what I'm sure you'll agree is an entirely proportionate response to having to drink from a slightly different cup, Grenville and his men 'burnt, and spoiled [the villagers'] corn, and town, all the people being fled'.

You'll be happy to note that later on, in a separate attack, Manteo's mum was also killed by the English.

WE SHIT DIRECTLY INTO OUR WATER SUPPLY AND DEALT WITH THE RESULTING CHOLERA DEATHS ONLY WHEN THE SMELL STARTED TO GROSS OUT MPs

In the mid-1800s, London was disgusting.

From the start of the century till 1850, the population rose from 1 million to 3 million, and we didn't have the matching sewage system to cope with the amount of poo this population had stockpiled inside of them. As well as that, our good friend the flushable toilet had just been introduced in wealthier households. This sounds like an improvement, but in reality this meant a quite literal shit tonne of piping hot human waste was being pumped directly from the bums of the rich into a river that doubled as the water supply for the city. We were shitting in our own mugs on an industrial scale, and wondering why we were getting ill.

As well as this, 'runoff' from slaughterhouses and factories were also pumped directly into the river, clearly thinking 'fuck it, why not at this point'. In the same way it's not possible to polish a turd, there is the advantage that you can't really make a turd look any turdier than a turd is.

In 1855 scientist Michael Faraday took paper down to the Thames to dip it in as a test. He described the river as looking like 'an opaque pale brown fluid',[11] which is polite Victorian scientist talk for 'poo'. Consequently, cholera epidemics kept on hitting the city. Between 1831 and 1854, thousands of Londoners were killed in massive epidemics caused by contaminated water.

The smell had been getting bad throughout the 1850s. Charles Dickens wrote to a friend, 'I can certify that the offensive smells, even in that short whiff, have been of a most head-and-stomach-distending nature.' At the time, most people* believed cholera was caused by the smells, and London reeked. Urgent action was needed. Which is why nothing was done until the smell started to gross out the wealthy.

In the summer of 1858, there was a horrendous heatwave. For two months, human and animal waste in the Thames fermented, causing an unforgettable stink. 'Gentility of speech is at an end,' the *City Press* wrote of it. 'It stinks, and whoso once inhales the stink can never forget it and can count himself lucky if he lives to remember it.'[12]

For the thousands shitting themselves to death from cholera epidemics over and over again, luck was finally in hand. The Houses of Parliament had just been rebuilt by the Thames, and at long last the stench was grossing out people who could take action. After trying to put a plaster over the problem by coating the Parliament curtains in chloride of lime (turbo bleach) and covering their mouths with handkerchiefs, MPs gave in and ordered the creation of a better sewer system, which went on to save thousands of lives. We finally dealt with the cholera deaths because politicians found work too pongy.

Bar a few, such as scientist John Snow (not that one) who in 1854 broke a water pump of a supply he suspected was infected with cholera, stopping an epidemic and helping to prove that it was waterborne. He died in 1858, well before his theory was widely accepted in 1866.

WE WENT TO WAR OVER A FANCY STOOL

In the late part of the 19th century, we decided to go to war with the Ashanti Empire in Ghana. In 1896, we basically crushed the Ashanti and banished their ruler, King Prempeh, and confiscated (nicked) all his treasures – bar one – and displayed them in our museums at home. The Ashanti had hidden a golden stool.

Whilst most people would look at a massive bag of swag we'd taken and think, 'well this seems fair enough, it's not really ours anyway no need to be greedy,' the British couldn't let it go. We had a lovely spot in the British Museum that would be perfect for a massive golden chair and we weren't about to let it go to waste.

Sir Frederick Hodgson, Colonial Secretary of Gold Coast, was determined to get it. In 1899, Fred sent a secret expedition to find the stool. They didn't find it, but they did make the new Ashanti leaders suspicious that they were going to try and swipe the chair again. Tensions rising, Fred asked for a meeting.

On 28 March 1900, the Ashanti welcomed the Secretary and a small group of soldiers into the city of Kumasi, even going to the lengths of having the city's children sing God Save the Queen to his wife. However, when he was seated, Hodgson noticed he had been sat on a regular, noticeably and insultingly, non-gold chair.

He got up and made one of the weirdest speeches ever to have preceded a war.

'Where is the Golden Stool? Why am I not sitting on the Golden Stool at this moment? I am the representative of the paramount power in this country; why have you relegated me to this chair? Why did you not take the opportunity of my coming to Kumasi to bring the Golden Stool and give it to me to sit upon?'[13]

The Golden Stool, whilst for us Brits a cool place to park our cheeks, was sacred to the Ashanti. Only the ruler was allowed to touch it, and even they didn't sit on it. During ceremonies, the stool was given its own throne to sit on, and the King sat next to it like an equal. They believed the stool to contain the spirits of their ancestors as well as those Ashanti yet to be born.

So from the Ashantis' perspective Frederick's big speech roughly translated as: 'Where is your sacred throne? Why am I not rubbing my ass on the ghosts of your ancestors and future generations right now? Why in the shit am I sitting on a normal chair when I could be parking my buttcheeks on your god?' It's like telling someone in modern times that you want to have a quick slash on their nan's grave, when there are plenty of perfectly serviceable toilets available.

The Ashanti didn't take kindly to this slight, and upon Fred's departure the Warrior Queen Yaa Asantewaa I began assembling the troops. At which point we backed down, realising they wanted it more and it was just a fancy chair to us. Ok, that was an obvious lie: we went and looked for the stool nearby, making the Ashanti even madder. They chased us, but we were able to flee and set up defences in the nearby British offices in Kumasi, where they held us under siege. Then we brought in several thousand soldiers to deal with the situation, escalating the situation a bit more for good measure.

Until the end of September, we attacked the Ashanti with gusto, with casualties running into the thousands, all because we wanted a fancy-ass golden chair. The Ashanti lost the war, and more of their leaders were exiled. But we never did get to sit on the golden stool.

TENS OF THOUSANDS HAVE DIED IN OUR CONCENTRATION CAMPS, WHICH DOESN'T SEEM LIKE THE ACTIONS OF A GREAT COUNTRY IF I'M HONEST

It's just awkward, isn't it? Because we don't half bang on about being the heroes of the Second World War, to the point that children probably think the Nazis invented concentration camps. But, as you've probably got the message by now, we are also cunts.

One of the most horrifying use of concentration camps by the British was during the Second Boer War. Set up in 1900, they were originally created as refugee camps to care for starving civilian families who had been forced to flee their homes. Which sounds charitable, if you ignore that the reason they were starving and fleeing was because we had burned their crops to the ground and slaughtered all their livestock. The British had instigated a 'scorched earth' policy in South Africa under Field Marshal Herbert Kitchener, in order to deal with guerrilla fighters. Civilian farms were burned in order to cut off the food supply of the guerrillas, incidentally cutting off the food supply of literally everyone else in the process.

Survivors, soldiers and civilians alike, were moved to concentration camps. Eventually there were 45 tented camps for Boer and 64 for black Africans prisoners, containing around 115,000 people in total.

There are a lot of reasons why we don't naturally burn all our crops and move ourselves to crowded tent villages, as we soon found out. Disease, starvation and exposure killed men, women and children at an alarming rate in these camps quite soon after they were set up.

Emily Hobhouse, a British welfare campaigner, visited some of the camps, finding inhumane conditions and disease, and during her time personally witnessing the deaths of several children. She then left those camps and discovered even worse camps. In one harrowing account, she told of Lizzie van Zyl, a child who died as a result of her time at the Bloemfontein Concentration Camp. Lizzie had been treated harshly, and put on distressingly low rations. Starving, she was moved to a hospital, where she was called an idiot by the staff for not speaking English. Hobhouse described how the girl had been calling out for her mother one day and an Afrikaner woman went to comfort her, only to be told not to because the child was a nuisance.

Hobhouse came back horrified and determined to spread the word of the torment and untold human suffering she had seen. When she did, she was met with open hostility from the media and government, who branded her a Boer-sympathising turncoat traitor for saying, 'hey wouldn't it be nice if the people we're imprisoning had liveable conditions or maybe just some soap.'

It took tireless campaigning by the Liberals in order to force an investigation, which then led to attempts to improve the camps before they were closed. During this time, between June 1901 and May 1902 nearly 28,000 people died in the camps, about 22,000 of whom were children.

If you think we learned the very obvious lesson here of 'concentration camps are bad' you are mistaken. In one harrowing example, the British government held over 50,000 Jewish people, most of whom were Holocaust survivors, in internment camps in Cyprus shortly after the Holocaust. After around 400 people died in those camps we learned our lesson though. I kid, we went on to use them one more time during the Mau Mau uprising in Kenya in the 1950s, leading to well over 100,000 deaths.

WE ROBBED PEOPLE'S GRAVES SO MUCH WE HAD TO BOOBY TRAP GRAVEYARDS WITH AUTOMATIC SHOTGUNS

There's nothing the British love more than tutting at people standing on the left of escalators in London, and desecrating the final resting place of the dead.

Doctors in the UK have wanted corpses to gawp inside since around AD 300. Just because doctors didn't know anything back then doesn't mean we didn't need to root around in a corpse before declaring, 'yeah I'll probably just put a lot of leeches on their testicles and if it's a real emergency maybe I'll drill a hole in their face'.

For centuries though, the religious views of the British prevented doctors from practising on cadavers in the open. Until the 14th century, messing around with corpses for medicine (or fun) was outlawed entirely, and well up until the mid-1700s, dissection was allowed only on hanged criminals. Which was a massive problem if you were a doctor who needed to learn how bodies work, and an even bigger one if you chose to specialise in necks.

Surgeons would often have a hard time getting bodies from the hangman and have to hand over bribes. Because even people who killed people routinely for a living thought it was ethically a bit iffy.

And so a dark industry of organised graverobbers sprung up. By the late 18th century, there was a thriving black market specialising in corpses. Gangs of graverobbers supplied anatomists with corpse after corpse, only slowing down when they wanted to control the supply in order to keep the prices up.

It got out of hand pretty quickly. Shakespeare's grave even spared a line to ward off potential graverobbers, reading 'cursed be he that moves my bones' instead of, for instance, mentioning his wife – and he didn't even die in the grave robbing heyday.

Two body snatchers in Edinburgh, William Burke and William Hare, got impatient waiting for people to die in order to get a paycheck, and killed sixteen people themselves in order to sell the bodies to anatomists. The problem got so bad that an industry also sprung up to stop grave robbers from robbing graves. Rich people could afford mortsafes – giant iron cages to house the dead that would prevent robbers from getting in – or hired people to stand guard until the body had rotted enough that it was no longer useful to surgeons. Like a bouncer but for your grandma's coffin.

Then there were booby traps. There are reports of cemetery guns being in regular use across England and Scotland to protect the dead: guns hooked up to tripwires and loaded with rock salt, pepper shot or plain old lethal ammunition. One way or the other, those doctors were getting a corpse.

Still undeterred, grave robbers would pose as mourners and widows to scope out the cemetery during the day, whilst gravekeepers would, in turn, wait until dark to lay their booby traps down.

Meanwhile the poor had to rely on placing stones and flowers on their loved ones' graves to detect disturbances (and then, I guess, just kind of note 'oh hey they dug up Janice' afterwards).

WE COMPENSATED SLAVERS WITH PILES OF CASH BUT GAVE NOTHING TO THE FREED SLAVES

In 1833, the British government decided to do the right thing and abolish slavery throughout the Empire.

The government passed the Slavery Abolition Act, which immediately freed slaves under the age of six and rebranded anyone over that age 'apprentices'. They were still slaves for 40.5 hours a week, but were allowed to spend the rest of their time if they weren't too knackered from being a sla—(sorry, apprentice) working elsewhere, in order to 'learn' how to be free.

By 1840 these 'apprentices' were actually freed for real this time, no longer required to work for their captors. Not being used to doing (eventually) the right thing (see all of British history thus far) the British government decided to be dicks one last time and compensate the slave owners but not the newly emancipated, more often than not penniless, slaves.

The government paid out £20 million to 3,000 slave-owners (worth around £2,300,000,000 in today's money) whilst around 800,000 slaves received a pat on the back and a 'go on then, off you fuck', which you'd have difficulty trading for food.

£20 million at the time, to put it lightly, was a buttload of money. The government borrowed this money (40 per cent of their national budget) to pay off slave owners, and we paid it off only 182 years later in 2015.

Until that point, any descendants of slaves (who, remember, never received a penny in compensation) paying taxes in the UK will have paid off sorry-we're-taking-your-property-away money to the people who kept their ancestors as slaves.

It just goes to show that even when we try to do the right thing, we're so out of practice we still end up being bellends for nearly 200 years afterwards.

WE WERE ROYAL SHITS TO PRISONERS AND ONCE FORGOT A PRISONER TO DEATH

Ye olde Britain used some brutal methods of torture on prisoners. As well as the usual run-of-the-mill stretching people till their bones dislocated or broke on the rack, and covering them with boiling hot tar and sticking feathers to the wounds, we got distressingly creative with our torture methods, and even our royalty got in on the action.

Henry VIII, for instance, made boiling people alive a legal form of capital punishment for swindlers, people who forged coins and those who killed people with poison.

King James VI of Scotland aka King James I of England *personally* watched over the torture of some of the most heinous types during the North Berwick witch trials. During these trials he gawped as people were forced to confess to witchcraft, which doesn't even exist, by having their fingernails removed and iron pins put in, having an assortment of appendages crushed with a specially designed vice, and crushing their feet with special boots to the point that they were so tiny they were useless as feet. This was on top of the usual strangulation, burning, sleep deprivation and good old classic dismemberment.

I know you're thinking 'it was different times and torture was seen as acceptable, so you can't judge them to be bellends using today's standards'. Well congratulations, you just defended opening up someone's belly with a knife and then letting a rat loose on their intestines, and making people into human soup. Feel proud of yourself?

As well as the more horrible methods of torture, which it's too grim to focus on for too long, we also showed a callous disregard for the welfare of our prisoners. You might think it's bad when you forget to turn the gas off – and it is, stop leaving your gas on or you're going to blow up your house. But so much worse is the time Sir Thomas Swinburne forgot someone to death in the 16th century.

Archibald Armstrong, a member of the Armstrong clan, was captured alive during a food raid and imprisoned in Thomas' castle in Haughton. Whilst waiting for a decision on Archibald's punishment from the courts, Thomas agreed to look after him. But then Thomas sort of got distracted from providing his prisoner with food. He was called away for a meeting with Cardinal Wolsey in York, and rode off to meet him, delegating the task of looking after his prisoner to a servant.

Then, after riding for three days, he had a bit of a feel around in his pocket and found (oh god) the only key to Archibald's cell.

Thomas, who to be fair to him was forgetful but not a complete bellend, turned his horse around immediately. Though it had been more than enough time without water to kill Archibald, he rode as fast as he could back to the castle, probably checking his other pockets to see if he'd murdered anyone else to death by mistake. Thomas claimed he rode the horse so hard the horse died. This was turning into a bit of a spree. He bought and rode a second horse, which survived and took him back to the castle.

He arrived around midnight and opened the dungeon cell. Inside was most of Archibald, minus a chunk of flesh in his arm where he'd gnawed at it for food. Archibald had been sat there, forgotten but not gone, for several days before he ate parts of his own famously strong arm, and was finally 'I've brought the wrong keys'-ed to death.

WE'VE TRICKED THE WORLD INTO THINKING OUR UPPER CLASSES ARE DIGNIFIED

Conservative peer Julian Fellowes has done an excellent job of convincing everyone our posh were polite and dignified types. Over six series of *Downton Abbey* he spread the word to 120 million people the world over that the British upper classes were classy, affable gentlemen and gentlewomen who would do anything for their servants.

In reality, the well-off over the centuries have been littered with wankers.

Gangs of poshos roamed the streets beating the crap out of people for fun

There are reports of a troupe of poshos calling themselves the Mohocks going around in the early 18th century, attacking men and women in London. According to several accounts, the group of well-off criminals stalked the streets rolling women down hills in barrels and mutilating people's faces, as well as cutting off noses and hands, spawning the phrases 'that escalated quickly' and 'hey what are you doing to my nose you bellend'. They were reportedly so rich they didn't even bother mugging their defence- and nose-less victims afterwards.

Spring-heeled Jack

From around 1837 onwards, people kept reporting sightings of a creature, sometimes with horns and fiery eyes, leaping over rooftops and over hedges and scaring the shit out of women. Several of the more grounded reports said that a tall thin man in a cloak and 'gentlemanly' appearance cornered women and clawed at them a bit at night. All the accounts end with Jack leaping away from his crimes like some sort of dickhead rabbit.

The smaller attacks turned into an urban legend, and reports about a satanic figure flying around London and the rest of the UK persisted until the 1880s.

A letter sent to the mayor after the initial attacks claimed that a group of aristocrats were doing it as a bet. E. Cobham Brewer, a companion of known 'prankster' (bellend) aristocrat Henry de La Poer Beresford, named Henry as Spring-heeled Jack after his death, saying that he used to jump out at travellers to amuse himself, and other gentlemen 'pranksters' (bellends) took up the torch.

Horse Nandos Jack

John 'Mad Jack' Mytton (bloody nominative determinism again) once rode his horse up the stairs to the Bedford Hotel in Leamington Spa, then cantered it through the restaurant and leapt over diners and the balcony onto the street for a bet.

I should probably mention that he was also a sheriff. Whilst not specifically prohibited by him being the Sheriff of Merionethshire, there's an argument that recklessly ploughing a horse through the 19th-century equivalent of Bella Italia at least goes against the spirit of the job. Amazingly, nobody was injured.

That incident was soon forgotten after he showed up to a dinner party riding a bear. At some point he decided the bear wasn't going fast enough (if you're looking for speed, maybe ride a horse) and kicked it. It objected to this and tore a chunk out of his calf. To be fair to John, 'please call a doctor, this fucking bear I rode here has eaten a part of my leg' is a hell of an entrance to a dinner party. There would be no awkward pauses in polite conversation that couldn't be filled with 'so I rode a bear here and the bastard ate me before I could park'.

WE EXECUTED HUNDREDS OF PEOPLE WITH CANNONS. *CANNONS.*

When another country executes prisoners, Britons like to look at them and say, 'well that's barbaric, how ghaaaastly' and have our butlers fetch the fainting couch. In the past, however, we were all for strapping prisoners to cannons and firing their torsos over as big a distance and radius as possible.

Hundreds of years after it was first used as a method of execution by the Mughal Empire, in the 17th century the British took up the mantle. At first we did it, oddly enough, because it was more humane than flogging people to death in countries we'd invaded where that was the current practice. Eventually, of course, we started using it for evil.

Muslims believed a man so destroyed couldn't get into Paradise, and Hindus believed that it destroyed the soul as well as the body. So we used it as a way of reassuring them that – as well as being killed in what I can only imagine was a very painful way – they were *also going to be punished after death*.

We had used this horrific method of execution on and off for most of a century, before getting cannon fever in the 1850s. In 1857, during the Indian Rebellion against the East India Company, we started firing people like we were Sir Alan Sugar.

One account of the end of a battle tells of how the British captured 300 prisoners. To stamp out the 'mutiny', we took prisoners and 'tied them together six at a time, placing them with their backs towards half a dozen guns, and at a little distance from them ... Every time the word was given to fire, thirty-six of them were blown to pieces. This was repeated over and over again, and as the heaps accumulated, we drew the guns back and continued till the men were all destroyed.'[14]

We killed only one European using this method. I guess it sucks the fun out of it for the Brits if the executed isn't soiling themselves with fear that they'll be damned for all eternity afterwards.

THERE ARE REPORTS THAT WE MAY HAVE HUNG A MONKEY. A *MONKEY.*

According to legend, during the Napoleonic Wars a French ship was wrecked just off the shore of Hartlepool. The locals rushed out to the shore to check out the wreck. There were no survivors, except for one. He was short, dressed in a full French army uniform and also he was a monkey.

According to the local myths (and a rather too upbeat song given the topic of monkeycide) the locals had never seen a monkey nor a Frenchman, and decided to put whatever it was they'd found on trial right there on the beach. Since the monkey wouldn't answer any questions on the grounds that it was a monkey, the locals decided that the monkey must be in cahoots with the French.

The monkey, which wasn't even given proper legal representation, was sentenced to death, and *was* hung using the mast of the boat on which it had served as the ship's entertainment. And so, according to the legend, that's how a monkey in a uniform was hung by the British.

It is, to be fair, clearly untrue, but it does reveal a few things about who we are as a people. For one, there is the possibility that the legend began because a young boy on the boat, a 'powder-monkey' hired to prime the cannons, was hung. Which granted would mean we aren't monkey killers – but 'oh no I can assure you the crime was more fucking heinous than that, your honour' is not the most effective defence in a monkey-murder trial.

It's also very possible* that this was all just made up by a rival town, to smear them as the kind of people who upon seeing an adorable monkey in a full navy uniform would try the bastard and hang it. Which would make us bellends in a slightly different way, just not of the monkey-hanging variety.

Weirdly the term 'monkey hangers' is now worn with pride by many locals, and is the nickname of several local sports teams. So even if we didn't hang a monkey, we've incorrectly identified the act of hanging monkeys as something worthwhile to list on our CVs.

*almost certain.

IRISH FAMINE (PART 2): TO JUSTIFY SENDING FAMINE RELIEF TO *A COUNTRY WE HELPED GIVE FAMINE TO*, WE MADE THEM BUILD ROADS THAT WENT NOWHERE

Putting Malthusianism – the idea that you should just let populations die until they reached a sustainable level – into practice required a strong dose of not giving a shit about the Irish. Fortunately the colonial administrator in charge of famine relief to Ireland, Sir Charles Trevelyan, had that in spades. Spades which he definitely wouldn't give to the Irish even if it was the only way of getting them food.

As well as believing that the best way to help the Irish was to not help them at all, he also didn't really want to help. Charlie believed that 'the judgement of God sent the calamity to teach the Irish a lesson, that calamity must not be too much mitigated'[15] and he had every intention of cosying up to this vengeful God.

He thought that the free market would find a solution, and was unwilling to intervene. We couldn't just give starving people food, he believed. Imagine what a precedent it would set if we started giving out free pasta just because an eighth of the population was dying in a famine we'd helped to cause. They'd probably start faking the medical symptoms of severe malnutrition in order to get some free linguine. What little relief we did give was given reluctantly, and with many caveats*. In essence, we used the Poor Laws to make sure some people were fed, but sure as hell wished they weren't.

The principle of getting people to work for below market pittances when they couldn't find regular work was already established. The problem was that there were so many people in Ireland without jobs (farms were bankrupt) or food (see previous brackets where I explained that farms were bankrupt). So rather than just giving starving children the food like some kind of commie, Charles authorised finding unnecessary building projects for the starving masses to work on. And so began the famine roads. We made the Irish build pointless roads that led from nowhere, to nowhere, in order to give starving people something to do in return for aid.

Charles's policy led to the building of odd, nonsensical roads that can still be seen almost 170 years later. With the money they earned from building them, it's been calculated that many workers were unable to buy enough food to make up the energy lost from building the roads. By the end of December 1846, 500,000 men, women and children were at work to build pointless stone roads for nobody in the middle of nowhere for enough money to buy not quite enough food to live on.

After the famine ended, with 1 million Irish people dead and 1 million emigrated, Charles was made a Knight Commander for his work.

*To be fair, some Brits did try to help unconditionally. Queen Victoria sent £2,000. Although she also convinced the Sultan of the Ottoman Empire to reduce his donation to £1,000 from £10,000 so that her donation didn't seem stingy, making her contribution a net loss of £7,000.

WE HIRED PIRATES TO GO BEAT THE CRAP OUT OF THE SPANISH IN PEACETIME

The British have a reputation (at least in films and Captain Pugwash) of being the noblemen of the seas, sailing around and fighting pirates, which is entirely unearned as we had our own state-sanctioned pirates named the Sea Dogs, who we hired to beat the crap out of Spanish sailors during peacetime.

Queen Elizabeth I authorised a group of essentially state-sponsored pirates, who were also slavers (of course) to steal from the Spanish as long as she got a cut of the booty. They were allowed to carry the 'Letters of Marque', a licence to attack and capture other vessels. It was essentially like James Bond's licence to kill, if James Bond was just some random thief rather than a spy, and had open intentions to use it purely for the purposes of being a prick.

The idea was the Sea Dogs would sail around the Atlantic and Caribbean stealing money from the Spanish and reducing their navy size at the same time. The Queen was worried about imminent war with the Spanish, probably provoked somewhat by the kind of moves such as legalising killing the Spanish for booty.

Amongst the Sea Dogs were some of the most famous sailors in history, including Sir Walter Raleigh and Sir John Hawkins. The most notorious, however, was Sir Francis Drake, who you probably know as defeating the Spanish Armada, and being the second person to circumnavigate the globe. He achieved this remarkable latter feat by robbing the Spanish at every available opportunity, travelling up the west coast of South America ransacking Spanish ports and commandeering ships. Not just a prick whilst at sea, he would also pull into Caribbean ports and demand money. He would then burn down parts of the city until he received whatever ransom he'd set. For this he earned the nickname El Draque, or The Dragon.

During one trip he captured the town of St Augustine in Florida, defended it for a few days from attack by Spanish and Native Americans, looted it a bit and then burned the whole town to the ground, including all the crops.

Another time, he and his men stopped off briefly to get into a fight with the indigenous residents of southern Patagonia, becoming the very first Europeans to slaughter these particular natives mercilessly.

Seven months after he returned from his Spanish murder tour, he was knighted for his efforts in the field of setting fire to Spanish towns and boats, somewhat to the irritation of the King of Spain.

WE SHOT AT A CROWD OF PEACEFUL PROTESTORS AS THEY FLED AND STOPPED FIRING ONLY WHEN WE RAN OUT OF AMMO

On 13 April 1919, a group of unarmed Punjabi civilians gathered in the public gardens of Jallianwala Bagh to peacefully protest against something else shitty we had done, whereupon they were shot in droves as they tried to flee the British troops who were armed to the teeth.

Earlier that day, Acting Brigadier-General Reginald Dyer banned meetings in the region in order to try and quell any demonstrations. We had recently deported several Indian politicians for being anti British Empire, and feared people rebelling against the move. Reg's message, and the implied threat behind it, hadn't been widely disseminated, and so a crowd of around 6,000–20,000 (based on several conflicting estimates) showed up, partly to protest and partly just to celebrate the Sikh festival of Baisakhi.

Reg, hearing of this entirely peaceful gathering in a public garden on a festival day, ordered his troops to the garden in order to open fire on the crowd without warning. Without even a friendly 'HEY, WOULD YOU MIND LEAVING PLEASE?' or a warning shot, Reg and his troops entered through the main entrance to the park and stayed there, blocking the best available exit for anyone who wasn't a fan of getting shot at. And then the massacre began.

The soldiers of the 2nd/9th Gurkha Rifles, the 54th Sikhs and the 59th Sind Rifles, under the Brigadier-General's orders, shot at the crowd, concentrating their fire on the smaller gates through which people were attempting to flee, the densest part of the crowd. When people threw themselves on the ground, the riflemen merely aimed lower. We stopped firing only when ammo supplies were nearly depleted, after about ten minutes of non-stop slaughter of the unarmed.

As well as riflemen, Reg had brought machine guns mounted on vehicles, but left them outside, not because it is undeniably evil to mow down the public with machine guns, but because the entrances were too small for the vehicles to pass through. Turns out the only thing that can stop the British from reaching their true capacity for evil is basic physics.

Around 1,000 people were killed, with 1,100–1,500 wounded or severely wounded by the shots themselves or the crush as people tried to escape the shots through the smaller entrances that Reg hadn't blocked. Some jumped down a well in the gardens in order to escape the carnage. Others died later that night, as the curfew Reg had in place prevented people from moving the injured.

Reginald was later asked why he had blocked the main exits, and not given any kind of warning to the crowd. He told them his objective, 'was not to disperse the meeting but to punish the Indians for disobedience.'[16] Which would be easier to believe if some of these 'disobedient' Indians weren't six-month-old babies at the time.

Reg was initially praised by people in the House of Lords, though thankfully in the House of Commons they were less enthusiastic, and Churchill called it 'a monstrous event' that amounted to murder.

Some historians believe this was the turning point where the Empire started to ease up on the senseless killing, bar from a few 'oopsies' (such as that time we systematically killed 11,000–90,000 people in Kenya). Whilst that's probably not the case, it at least seems to have been the point when a lot of Indians loyal to the British abandoned the 'loyal to the British' part of their descriptors. The problem with shooting down a crowdful of peaceful protestors for showing support for anti-Empire leaders is you do sort of prove the leaders have a bit of a point about the Empire.

WE PLANNED TO ERADICATE THE NATIVE AMERICANS BY GIVING THEM BLANKETS

Smallpox was one of the deadliest viruses in human history, killing millions around the world in horrible agony. The infected developed massive fevers, blisters and scabs, vomited, got diarrhoea and had their immune systems crippled, which for many eventually led to their deaths. It's not something you'd wish on your own worst enemy. Unless you're British, of course, in which case knock yourself out.

During the Seven Years' War (1756–63) we tried to use smallpox as a biological weapon against the Native Americans, who weren't even close to our number 1 'worst enemy' list at the time.

When there was an outbreak of smallpox at one of our outposts, Fort Pitt, in 1763, Field Marshal Jeffery Amherst was told about the situation. Without pausing to remark, 'oh no how terrible, smallpox is bad,' like a regular human being, Jeffery saw the potential of weaponising the disease against the Native Americans holding us under siege at the fort. He authorised the use of smallpox-infected linen against them.

'Could it not be contrived to Send the Small Pox among those Disaffected Tribes of Indians?' He wrote to Colonel Henry Bouquet, in a Bond-villainesque message so badly coded you can practically hear the wink. 'We must, on this occasion, Use Every Stratagem in our power to Reduce them.'[17]

Bouquet replied and promised to give it a shot, taking careful steps not to infect himself whilst collecting a scab-filled blanket from an infected patient.

'You will do well to try to inoculate the Indians by means of blankets,' Jeffrey continued, going full-on Dalek this time, 'as well as to try every other method that can serve to extirpate this execrable race.'[18]

The blankets and a handkerchief were given as gifts to Native American diplomats during talks aiming to persuade the British to abandon the fort.

Though the Native Americans did have an outbreak during 1763-4, it's not known whether this was directly caused by our weaponised linen. It's unlikely they could spread the disease easily without transporting it in a biohazard fridge, which would raise suspicions somewhat even if fridges had been invented by that point. But it doesn't make us better as a people that we had the genocidal intent but not the adequate fridges to carry it out.

WE INTRODUCED HOMOPHOBIC LAWS TO THE WORLD THEN JUDGED THEM FOR BEING HOMOPHOBIC

The British get pretty judgy (and rightly so) of governments that still ban homosexual relationships. But of seventy-one countries around the world where it's illegal, over half of them are former British colonies. As much as it would be nice to sit back and say, 'what a wild coincidence, Lordy lordy really how odd, anyway must dash' – the reason for that is we put the laws there in the first place.

In over thirty of these countries, they are still using the original laws (or laws based on) the ones we put in place well over a hundred years ago. We may still feel prudish now (I for one won't look at the screen during *Game of Thrones* in case there are boobs, and instead treat it like an audiobook – don't pretend you don't do the same) but British Victorians were extremely repressed when it came to sex, and strongly felt they should impose this on other nations.

When we went around the world, we saw people who weren't adhering to our own repressed view of sexuality and decided that had to stop. It's like going to a foreign country on purpose and then complaining about how foreign it is when you arrive, which to be fair to the Victorians is an activity we still do.

British colonists at the time documented widespread homosexuality in the countries they were colonising. One explorer, Sir Richard Francis Burton, wrote about a 'Sotadic Zone' across Europe, North Africa, most of Asia and the entirety of North and South America where romantic-sexual relationships between men were many, allowed and celebrated. Which suggests that homosexuality laws were by no means something they themselves were screaming out for.

Britain, on the other hand *was* concerned with it. As well as feeling the need to 'correct' the natives' 'morals' (an odd thing to want to do when you don't exactly have the high ground as an invader ruling with massive cannons), we also introduced the laws to 'protect' ourselves and our soldiers and officials from being 'corrupted' by natives who might turn military camps into 'replicas of Sodom and Gomorrah'[19] whilst they were over there away from their wives. Essentially a big part of why homosexuality was outlawed in these countries was because we were worried we might like it.

The laws we put in place, starting in India as a test run before implementing them elsewhere, were terrible and helped shape attitudes for years to come. Not including ages of consent or consent itself in the law meant that gay consensual relationships were conflated with rape and paedophilia, both in terms of the law and later in terms of wider attitudes.

Towards the end of the Empire our own attitudes started (incredibly slowly) to shift in the right direction, but we let go of our colonies just before decriminalising homosexual relationships ourselves, leaving the laws in place throughout the former Empire.

We came in, we imposed laws against homosexuality that most of these places weren't calling for and we made people believe homosexuality was wrong. And then, harm already done, we changed our minds and judged them for not being liberal like us.

WE BURNED DOWN THE WHITE HOUSE TO SHOW THE AMERICANS HOW BATSHIT WE WERE

For all our notions of being a kindly nation interfering through warfare only when other countries really need our help, we're actually much more of what military strategists call 'a big vindictive shower of petty bastards who will fight you for looking at them funny'.

If there's anyone that can escalate a conflict needlessly, it's the British. A classic example of this was when we burned down the White House in a deliberately disproportionate retaliation to make them scared of what we'd do next.

In May 1814 the Americans* raided Port Dover, Ontario, where the British had stocks and grain stored for our troops. In response, the British governor of The Canadas (British colonies in Canada) ordered that our soldiers 'assist in inflicting that measure of retaliation which shall deter the enemy from a repetition of similar outrages [. . .] you are hereby required and directed to destroy and lay waste such towns and districts as you may find assailable.'[20]

With those instructions, troops led by Major General Robert Ross headed to Washington DC. During the brutal attack, President James Madison and his government fled the city, whilst the British remained behind. Having scared off the military and the whole government from the capital city, we had made our statement and could have left it at that. So we raided the White House (then known as the Presidential Mansion) before setting it on fire out of spite. We also burned the Capitol building and, just as a final 'yeah while I'm burning stuff', the Library of Congress for some reason too. Clearly we didn't want them to come back and read any books.

In the end, what stopped the rampage wasn't the realisation that 'hmmm now that I think about it, burning down the capital is a bit of an overreaction' but because a tornado hit the city, put out the fires and stopped us from lighting more. It turns out we're more destructive and slightly less ethically minded than a goddamn tornado.

*who not long before this were British and were clearly having trouble letting go of the habit of a lifetime of being massive bellends.

WE TRIED TO HOLD A **RIVER** HOSTAGE

In 1956, Britain and America reneged on a promise to help finance a dam in Egypt, out of fear of Egypt's ever growing ties with the Soviet Union. In response, Egypt went a bit commie, declaring martial law and taking control of their own Suez Canal.

Egypt then wanted to charge a toll on the canal, which had previously been owned by the British and French Suez Canal Company, in order to raise funds for the dam by themselves. The canal was an incredibly important shipping route for getting petroleum from the Persian Gulf to Europe. We weren't about to let a country THAT WE USED TO OWN treat us like this and started hatching a plan.

Bored of our usual tactic by this point of merely grabbing a shitload of weapons and killing every man, woman and child in sight, we decided on this occasion to go a bit Bond villainesque. We decided what we really wanted to do was to take the Nile as a hostage.

We still controlled Uganda at the time, where one of the sources of the Nile flowed through. The plan was to construct a dam in Uganda, which would stop 7/8ths of the water supply by the time it got to Egypt. Which given that this whole thing was started by our refusal to pay for a dam in the first place, was a bit of a dick move, even when you don't consider that you're also stealing a river from Kenya where the Nile also passed through.

The plan, which finally got declassified in 2006, did not *specifically* deny that they were planning on sending threatening cups of the Nile water to Egypt like a kidnapper would send a finger to prove the victim is still alive. Which I find quite sinister.

After much discussion, it was decided that we shouldn't go through with the cartoonishly evil plan for fear of a violent backlash. We decided instead to spread a rumour that we might be twatty enough to do it instead, and the Colonial Secretary (an actual ministerial role back then) Alan Lennox-Boyd gave a speech heavily implying we might just cut off their water.

Egypt were unconvinced, so instead we went back to our tried and thoroughly tested plan A – sending in the military in a way that broke international law.

The problem with just walking into the country and demanding the canal back is that being violent to a country we used to own for the crime of [checks notes] running their own canal tends to get those bores at the UN saying stuff like 'hey, please stop committing war crimes'. So between Britain, France and Israel we hatched another plot, in which Israel would invade the country, and we would waltz right in there with France under the guise of pretending to keep the peace.

Once we were in, we immediately began occupying the canal, taking it hostage the old-fashioned way, with big guns and absolutely no fucking shame. The UN, under pressure from the US, quickly put a stop to this when they realised we were up to our usual 'taking stuff that doesn't belong to us' shenanigans.

Old habits, just like everyone who gets in the way of the British and petrol, die hard I guess.

WE THINK WE'RE SO SCIENCEY, BUT WE ONCE EXECUTED A MURDERER THEN ELECTROCUTED HIS CORPSE FOR AN HOUR TO TRY TO BRING HIM BACK TO LIFE

From the 17th century onwards, Britain had a reputation as a place of science and enlightenment. But we were also delightfully whacky bellends in the name of – and I'm using it very loosely here and might even use three or four quotation marks – """"""science"""""".

Hot air ballooning to space

In September 1862, astronomer James Glaisher and buddy set off in a hot air balloon in a misguided attempt to get to space.

When they hit four miles, the pigeons they'd brought along with them started dying, their first clue that maybe they hadn't thought things through. They then both experienced the bends, and lost control of most of their limbs, and were only able to descend again when Glaisher's companion Henry Coxwell yanked at the valve release cord with his teeth.

Back on the ground, the only surviving pigeon was traumatised and wouldn't leave Glaisher's hand for fifteen minutes. They thought they were pioneering scientists heading to space, but it turned out they were just two idiots killing and scaring the shit out of birds.

Doctor-recommended children's cough syrup was basically just smack

In Victorian England we would very much rather get ill kids smacked up on morphine than listen to them cough, and so scientists invented cough medicine to do just that. Morphine, chloroform, codeine, more morphine, powdered opium, cannabis and heroin were all ingredients in 'Children's Soothing Syrup' the 19th-century equivalent of Calpol. But you should see their 6+ version.

Electrocuting orphans for publicity

In the 1730s, astronomer Stephen Gray showed off electrical flow by grabbing a quick orphan from the orphanage, suspending him in mid-air with insulating cords and then electrifying him by rubbing him with glass tubes until he produced sparks. Another scientist, Nicholas Joseph Callan, conducted his experiments on his students, hospitalising one and knocking another unconscious. When he was banned from experimenting on the students, he switched to live chickens.

Electrocuting corpses for fun

On the 4 November 1818 a theatre full of medical gawpers gathered round at the University of Glasgow, and waited for a man to be executed. Convicted murderer Matthew Clydesdale was hung and transported by Glasgow police to the theatre, where Scottish *geologist* Andrew Ure proceeded to drain the body of blood for half an hour before hooking the body up to a massive electric battery in a misguided attempt to bring the body back to life.

'Every muscle in his countenance was simultaneously thrown into fearful action; rage, horror, despair, anguish, and ghastly smiles, united their hideous expression in the murderer's face,'[21] Ure wrote of the experiment, before continuing to electrocute the corpse for three quarters of an hour. The attempt to resuscitate Clydesdale, obviously, failed. Andrew chalked it up as a slight win, as he realised if he had been successful he would have technically brought a murderer back to life, which would have been even more morally 'iffy' than what he'd just done to an unconsenting corpse in front of a packed audience of looky loos.

WE WERE PEAK COLONIAL WANKERS IN NEW ZEALAND

We've always loved New Zealand, even before archaeologists discovered that's where the events of *Lord of the Rings* took place. Problem was that even though it was largely uninhabited when we 'found' it (discounting sheep and the 18th-century equivalent of gap-year students) it wasn't quite uninhabited enough for our tastes. We tried to rectify this during colonisation through ridiculously unbalanced warfare, provoking the Māori into unnecessary conflicts, and just generally being irritating dicks to the point that most people would think, 'ah sod it, let's risk all the poisonous death spiders and just move to Australia'. Let's take a closer look:

Absurdly unbalanced warfare

The conflicts we've had with indigenous populations of various countries we fancied for ourselves have always been fairly imbalanced and this was no exception. During the invasion of Waikato, we sent some 18,000 British troops, assisted by artillery, cavalry and local militia, to fight 4,000 basically naked Māori rebels basically armed with spears. It's like setting up a boxing match between a particularly weedy toddler and Muhammad Ali. The Māori put up a good fight, creating anti-artillery bunkers and fighting a guerrilla-style war, but in the end they were massively overpowered. Never bet on the people waving a stick at a cannon. After thousands of the Māori had died, we confiscated more land from the survivors as punishment for their rebellion. By a wild coincidence, the land was what we wanted in the first place.

Particularly dickish land-appropriating tactics

We used a whole load of tricksy methods to get land from the Māori. The New Zealand Company (a British company with the goal of colonising New Zealand) just straight up created false deeds to blocks of land, and then fought the Māori when they protested when the company tried to clear them off the land. Other land purchases were, at best, incredibly dubious.

Then in the New Zealand Settlements Act 1863 we legalised land confiscation from any Māori tribes we considered in rebellion against the British. This annoyed the Māori, who would then fight against it, thus becoming 'in rebellion' against the British, justifying more ~~theft~~ *perfectly legal confiscation*. We would then sell the land we ~~stole~~ *confiscated legally* from rebels and use it to fund fighting against more rebels.

We got into a fight over a flag

In 1845 we started a war with the Māori by putting up our flag in the town of Kororareka. When the local chief chopped it down, we put it back up again. And again. And again. After the fifth time the flag was chopped down, rather than just accept this was one city where it's best to stay flagless, we let it escalate to a bloody full-scale one-month warfare in which around 160 people died over a little wavy bit of cloth.

We introduced guns

We, along with other European bellends, introduced guns to New Zealand. This turned local fights between Māori tribes with relatively low casualty rates into much bigger bloodbaths. But in our defence, we got quite a bit of land out of the trade.

WE USED TO TREAT PEOPLE WHO HAD COMMITTED SUICIDE LIKE VAMPIRES

There can't be many things more distressing than learning a loved one has taken their own life. Unless, of course, someone then came round and announced they were going to take that loved one and ram a stake through their heart at midnight and dump them in a pit at a crossroads in a big pile of assorted executed murderers. Which is what we did in England right up until 1822.

In the 13th century 'self-murder' became a crime. In order to be convicted you needed to be deemed dead and sane. Once that was 'proven' to the satisfaction of the Crown, they would then punish your body by burying you alongside actual murderers, and also punish your family by taking all their (and your) belongings. Along with being depressed and having suicidal thoughts, you would be burdened with the knowledge that if you were to attempt suicide you could leave your entire family completely destitute as well as heartbroken.

What happened to your body after suicide – stake through the heart and thrown into a pile of bodies at midnight – was exactly the same treatment given to executed murderers.

It's not clear why we would bury both murderers and suicides at crossroads. There are theories that it was a kindness – because the people buried there were not allowed any kind of religious ceremony as they were interred – but they at least got a sort of cross, albeit quite a roady one. Other theories suggest that it was a superstition, and they were placed at crossroads to confuse any returning ghosts. Although with the whole of eternity ahead of them, it's hard to see how a ghost wouldn't get around to trying slightly more than three directions.

Eventually, following the widely discussed suicide of Lord Castlereagh in 1822, there were calls to stop the practice of burial at crossroads. People were beginning to become more understanding of mental illness, and the final crossroad burial took place the next year.

However, that wasn't the end of punishing people for attempting suicide, which remained illegal in England right up until 1958. Though prosecutions were rare, especially before the law was repealed, people were taken to trial at the lowest points in their lives, causing no end of stigma in front of their local communities. Of those that went to trial, many were dismissed with compassion, but a lot of others were slapped with a massive fine, and some were even sent to jail. Which even as a layperson, you can assume wouldn't be the ideal psychiatrist-recommended way to begin a recovery.

WE LET A LIAR LIE A LOT OF CATHOLICS TO DEATH

Britain likes to pretend it's an open and tolerant nation. But at one point in history we did kill a looooot of Catholics based on the words of a known liar rather than listen to their side of the story.

Titus Oates was a liar. During his early life he tried to become a vicar at uni, failed, pretended he had a degree anyway, changed his mind and decided he wanted to become a schoolmaster, then lied and accused the current schoolmaster of sodomy with a pupil in order to open up a vacancy.

Having been jailed for perjury and fled, he managed to get into a Jesuit house and started training to become a Doctor of Divinity. He was expelled for doing a bunch of blasphemy against God, which isn't normally behaviour you'd expect of someone who wants to be a holy man.

Returning to London angry at the Catholics who kicked him out, he teamed up with Israel Tonge, a fanatical anti-Catholic clergyman considered to be insane, even at the time. Together, they fabricated The Popish Plot, an entirely imaginary plot against the King (supposedly to be carried out by Catholics) that would see at least twenty Catholic people executed in some of the most horrible ways imaginable.

They wrote a gigantic document accusing the Catholic Church itself of authorising the assassination of King Charles II. They named nearly a hundred innocent Jesuits as being involved in the made-up plot to overthrow him and install Catholicism under Charles's brother James, before killing a whole pile of Protestants. Titus then snuck the manuscript into the house of a respected physician, with whom Israel was living. Israel then pretended to find the document the next day, and immediately informed people close to the King. If you think your flatmate is irritating when they steal your bread, try waking up and finding your housemate is attempting to get you executed for treason you didn't commit.

King Charles II dismissed the plot at first after he met Oates. He was unconvinced by him and thought him to be a teller of mistruths and a wicked man, which is 17th-century King talk for 'he's a "bit of a lying shit"'. However, he allowed an investigation due to the sheer volume of very specific accusations. Like how if someone said to you 'one of your colleagues has it out for you' you might dismiss it, but if someone says 'Sharon from accounts says she's going to shit in your lunchbox at 12:17' you might have a quick glance at Sharon and quietly nip out for a Pret.

On 28 September 1678, Titus made 43 accusations of plots against Catholics and 531 Jesuits, that he may have chosen at random, to the King's Privy Council, who believed him. On the strength of his testimony – he was a convincing liar – he was given a massive allowance, an apartment in Whitehall and his own squad of soldiers, and started rounding up Jesuits, including several who had been friends with him in the past.

Mad with power and capitalising on hysteria surrounding the murder of a Protestant-supporting MP (by an unknown person), Oates used the murder as further evidence for his made-up plot, and accused more people of being in on it. He discovered the English government would go along with just about any story as long as it was anti-Catholic.

WE AREN'T ABOVE DISGUISING OURSELVES AS CHINESE MERCHANTS IN ORDER TO STEAL TEA

As we've already established, there's nothing the British liked more in the 19th century than tea and stealing things that weren't ours. Robert Fortune and the British East India Company found a way of combining both loves whilst also mixing in our lesser-known third love of doing offensive impersonations of people with whom we had beef.

As discussed earlier in the book, in the 1840s China had a monopoly on the tea industry, and we'd do anything to get our hands on it. The First Opium War, where we attacked a friendly nation to make them accept opium in return for tea, made the British think that maybe we should find a back-up way of getting our tea-stained fingers on it.

The East India Company, ears pricking up when they heard there might be an opportunity to steal some shit, swooped in and recruited Scottish Botanist Robert Ford. They tasked Ford with getting samples of tea from China and transporting them to India, where they could grow the plant themselves without the hassle of having to pay money for it.

The main problem was that Chinese producers closely guarded the secrets of how they cultivated the plants. They were pretty much the only producers in the world, and it was (and still is) the earth's favourite drink. China forbade selling tea plants, and it was going to take a really batshit scheme to get the secrets from them. Saying 'hey would you mind us taking a look at that for a second' then cheesing it just wasn't going to work. This was going to take all of our cunning, as anyone who embarked on this mission would risk being flayed alive – the penalty for piracy at the time. Eventually, we shaved Robert and attached a fake lump of hair to the back of his bald head to make it look like a queue (the long, braided clump of hair favoured by the Qing dynasty at the time).

He then disguised himself as a Chinese merchant and moved around China, illegally travelling far away from the areas around the ports that Europeans were allowed in at the time. If anyone was to get suspicious of him and ask, e.g. 'why are you a full foot taller than the average Chinese person at the time we're currently living in' he would reply, genuinely, 'I am Chinese from a distant province beyond the Great Wall,' in a thick Scottish accent. Rather than risk angering an official, he'd find they would kowtow to him rather than question further, even though his accent was so strong he might as well have hit them with a rendition of Auld Lang Syne on the bagpipes.

He went off into the mountains, learning how to make tea at a time when China was so secretive we didn't even know that black tea and green tea came from the same plant. On his mission he was able to smuggle many young tea plants, seeds and tea-growers to India, breaking China's monopoly on tea and their entire tea-based economy in the process.

All because when people saw an obviously Scottish man dressed up as a Chinese person none of them thought they should report it – probably because it's not something you would expect a sane adult to do outside of cartoons.

WE BURNED THE RECORDS OF HOW AWFUL WE'VE BEEN THEN SMASHED UP THE ASHES

When Britain finally started to give back some of the countries we stole, we had a bit of a problem. We'd spent many decades being ruthless, racist shits and diligently documenting it in our own colonial records. Archives we'd now have to hand over to the new independent governments taking over. It's like if you're handing over your job to the new guy, and you're forced to confront the fact you spent a lot of your billable hours faxing racial slurs to that nice chap in accounts. You could tell your successor the truth to let them know the mess you've made, or you could spend your last few days on the job hiding the paper trail.

And so it came to our last days of the empire and, in a classic sign of innocence, we decided to burn all our documents in a massive fire – because we had nothing to hide we just like fires ok COLUMBO stop asking questions. Operation Legacy had begun.

Sometimes, we tried to limit ourselves to just destroying the racist stuff. In Northern Rhodesia, officials were ordered to destroy 'all papers which are likely to be interpreted, either reasonably or by malice, as indicating racial prejudice or religious bias on the part of Her Majesty's government'.[22] It appears a large portion of the documents read something along the lines of 'and then we done another bad racism' because a hell of a lot of papers suddenly went missing. In India we burned so much evidence that a 'pall of smoke'[23] fell over Delhi, probably spelling out one last racist epithet in the sky for old times' sake. And, in case you were worried, we weren't taking any chances: it was specified that, after burning our misdemeanours, 'the waste should be reduced to ash and the ashes broken up'[24]. We may never know what horrible things we've done in the past, but it appears that whatever it was we felt it was so toxic that it would embarrass us if the world even got hold of the soot.

We did this all over the world, from Borneo to Kenya. Some files were even placed in well-weighted crates and sunk in deep and current free water at the maximum practicable distance from shore'[25]. I'm not saying that we definitely destroyed damning evidence of crimes so heinous we could never be forgiven, but when you feel the need to drown your spreadsheets in the middle of the ocean, you've probably done something that would at least warrant a 'quick chat' with HR. It's not a great sign when you've done something so bad or racist it should only be read by fish.

And therefore, whatever you read in this book about how big of a bellend we were during the Empire, we'll never know precisely how big we really were. At this point, that can only be a good thing.

WE KILLED QUITE A LOT OF PEOPLE BY DRAWING A RANDOM LINE ON A MAP

Whilst the British have proved ourselves not very trustworthy with a gun over the years, it turns out if you want everyone to live you shouldn't really leave us alone with a pencil and a map.

From 1757 to 1858, India was ruled by the (British) East India Company, a cotton and tea company that strayed quite quickly from their mission statement and branched out into being brutal colonial dictators.

In 1857, the residents of India – Muslim and Hindu – got fed up of being ruled by what was essentially an evil version of Twinings, and rebelled. The uprising failed and it led to the British government directly ruling in India instead.

The British weren't a fan of lots of people uniting against us, and instigated our classic 'divide and rule' policy. The idea was to make local groups fight against themselves to stop them fighting us, making them easier to rule over. We paid Hindu speakers to speak against Muslims, and Muslims to speak against Hindus. When we allowed limited voting, we made people vote for candidates separately by religion. Muslims would vote for Muslims, Hindus for Hindus. And so, over many years, we stoked up a divide that wasn't really there before we'd arrived. By the time the Second World War came around, there was a large Muslim movement (The Muslim League) demanding to be given their own separate independent country, Pakistan.

When Britain, unable to rule any more, came to hand over power, we handled this situation we'd created with our characteristic application of not really giving a shit. We believed the nation was now too divided (because of us) to remain united without British rule, so it was decided we would divide it into two, creating the nation of Pakistan. We gave the delicate job of dividing it to someone with intricate knowledge of the area who had been there all their lives and allowed him several years to get it right.

I'm just kidding – we gave it to a man who had never travelled further east than Paris. He was then packed him off to India and given a deadline of five weeks to figure it all out. Cyril Radcliffe headed a border committee, with the goal of drawing a border that left minimal people on the 'wrong side'. We'll never know his entire reasoning behind why he squiggled the line where he did, as he burned his documents before he left the country, a day before the border was implemented. Radcliffe justified how quickly the job was done by stating that no matter what he did, people would suffer. Of that he was entirely correct.

The line was set. Millions of people were on the 'wrong' side in both directions. Muslims were in India, Hindus and Sikhs were in Pakistan. They desperately tried to flee to the other side of the border. Millions died in the chaos, either in violence as 14–16 million were displaced, or through disease in refugee camps after they crossed the border.

Having stoked up religious tension where there was none before over decades, Britain was responsible for the violence and misery. So, without wasting a moment, we fucked off whistling and left the new fledgling governments to deal with it. What would you expect from a nation happy to doodle people to death.

WE SENT FIVE WARSHIPS TO DEAL WITH A CRIME COMMITTED BY A PIG

There's a small island off the Canadian coast where, in 1859, we nearly went to war with America over a pig. Due to an ambiguous border agreement, both the US and UK thought that they owned the San Juan Islands, a strategically useful bit of land that both believed would give them control over an important shipping channel. The islands were already occupied, of course, but nobody gave a shit about that. Since neither the British nor the American settlers lived near the islands at the time, nobody thought about it much. But when both sides started edging their settlements closer, that's when it started to get tricky.

James Douglas, governor of British Columbia, wanted to keep the islands for the British, but he really didn't want to do anything drastic like actually live on them. To claim the island we definitely wanted and weren't just being dicks about, Douglas sent sheep. Over 1,000 were sent to the island, under the supervision of one British shepherd, Charles Griffin. Charles set up a sheep ranch in the disputed territory with the help of the native shepherds.

The Americans didn't like this, and sent a collector to try to tax Charles, who didn't like that very much either. Charles deputised one of the local shepherds and told him to arrest the American tax collector, Henry Webber. Henry didn't like being arrested by a farm boy who had just been promoted to deputy, and pulled a gun on him, which his three seconds of experience in the role and precisely fuck all training hadn't really prepared him for. After an awkward few moments, both sides backed away quietly.

Eventually, Americans started moving to the island and set up their own farms, turning the sheep conflict into a pig and cattle battle royale. Both sides set up farms and lived in a tense but polite standoff, until one day when an act so heinous happened that neither side could ignore: a British pig ate one of the Americans' potatoes. American Lyman Cutlar, naturally, took out his gun and shot the pig for the theft.

Lyman offered to pay $10 for the pig he'd killed. Charles demanded $100, which Lyman refused to pay on the grounds that the pig had been 'trespassing' because the British let it run freely like a cat. According to one account (which sounds a little too good to be true) the American told Charles, 'it was eating my potatoes', to which Griffin replied, 'it is up to you to keep your potatoes out of my pig'.[26]

It was a horrible incident, but one that could be solved through talking. So both sides brought in the military. The Americans shipped in 66 soldiers, whilst we brought in three warships full of soldiers, to wait menacingly just off shore. The Americans brought in 461 soldiers with 14 cannons, whilst we threatened them with five warships with 70 guns and 2,140 men. All ready to cannon the fuck out of each other if there was another pig murder.

The two sides stayed there for several weeks, making threats and insults at each other whilst the locals sat there confused and completely ignored. Before sense kicked in and both governments issued orders to stand down, one British military officer was threatening to 'make a Bunker Hill of it', referencing a previous battle between the two nations where thousands of people were injured or died. It's like having an argument with a spouse and bringing up the Battle of the Somme.

Eventually we ended up giving the islands to the Americans during talks, rendering the whole bizarre incident pointless. No more pigs were harmed. Except, of course, for the many hundreds of pigs that were crushed down into sausages.

WE REWROTE HISTORY ONLY MENTIONING THE GOOD BITS

Imagine if you would that *Eastenders* gets desperate for ratings and introduces a character based on Hitler. Now imagine he gets his own major story arc where he conks his head (clumsy Hitler!) and gets a specific type of soap-amnesia where he can remember only the good stuff he's done. He spends the whole week-run wondering why people in the Queen Vic are calling him a cunt and explaining to whoever is kicking the shit out of him at the time 'BUT I'M A GOOD GUY – I DON'T EVEN EAT MEAT' whilst Ian Beale cleans blood off his shoe.

Anyway, amnesia Hitler is basically us Brits.

Over the last few years, ranging anywhere from three to fifty, there's been a trend of politicians and media and people on the street taking credit for the good bits we've done in history and conveniently forgetting about all the atrocities. Politicians who weren't even close to being loaded into their fathers' penises yet, let alone being fired into their mums, somehow manage to use the pronoun 'we' when talking about defeating Hitler.

And yet suddenly we go all 'we aren't responsible for what our ancestors did' when reminded about one of our many massacres. In short, you can either be responsible for what our ancestors did or you can't. You can't just pick out the good bits and say 'we did that bit'.

We've made some very weird decisions lately and you could say that our selective memory of history and our idealised vision of our own place in the world is at least in part to blame. We're soap-amnesia Hitler deciding to leave the East End because he thinks everyone elsewhere absolutely loves him.

If we're ever going to move on and figure out what's best for our country as we are now, it's time we started remembering all the other stuff that takes us down a peg or two by reminding ourselves we're basically just bellends with top hats. And we don't even wear top hats any more.

I know you want to say 'but all these massacres are in the past', and 'we can't be held responsible for what our ancestors did', and that's fine. But in that case you don't get to say 'we saved you in the war' like it means anything unless you personally stormed the beach of Normandy as a sperm.

So, until we've solved our delusions of grandeur I propose that if we must allude to our glorious past we caveat it with:

'We're a great nation, we saved France in the Second World War. Of course we did fucking murder the Mau Mau like it was going out of fashion, so swings and roundabouts.'

Or, to be more exact:

'We helped to defeat Hitler. Mind you we did sort of twat the fucking life out of indigenous peoples of the world for profit for centuries, test nuclear weapons in Australia, realise there was more radiation than expected but decide not to tell Australia nor the nearby aboriginals, and we built ships for the confederates, one of our first forays into arming cartoonishly evil maniacs for money. Then there was that time King John took a trip around Ireland, and spent most of it pulling the beards of Irish kings and laughing hysterically at how annoyed they got. And of course we massacred and severely injured peaceful protestors at Peterloo because they wanted mild Parliamentary reforms. Also we sent all our orphans and criminals to Australia and told some of the orphans they were orphans but really they had parents. And that time we (repeatedly) caused genocides by legally installing hierarchies of ethnic groups where none existed beforehand, then arming them and then leaving the country saying 'whatever happens now is on you' and that time in the 18th century where we had a zoo and the price of admission was a live dog or cat that could be fed to the lions. Then we once started a war with the Māori in New Zealand by putting up our flag in the town of Kororareka. When the local chief chopped it down, we put it back up again. And again. And again. After the fifth time, rather than just accept this was one city where it's best to stay flagless, we let it escalate to a bloody full-scale 10 month warfare over a little wavy bit of cloth. Or that time we sent women to jail and force-fed them because they wanted a vote or that time when . . .

ACKNOWLEDGEMENTS

My biggest thanks, of course, goes to Britain for being the kind of bellend which makes filling a book of this type ridiculously easy.

Special thanks should also go to Emily Barrett from Little, Brown for editing down the thousands of times we were horrific maniacs into 52 readable (and occasionally even fun) times (and for having the brilliant idea in the first place, and giving me the chance to write it). My thanks to everyone else at L,B – from design to production – for getting the book off the ground, and to Emanuel Santos for the perfect illustrations.

Thank you to all my family and friends for keeping me going, my dad for telling me to keep writing when I wanted to give up, and Katie for always supporting me. Margaret-Anne Docherty for giving me my start in writing, and always pushing me to do more. My grandparents for always looking out for me, and David, who would have loved that I've got a funny book published on his favourite topic of history.

And a huge thanks to my Twitter friends and followers (without you this book would not exist) and my DM group, the name of which I cannot print because of obscenity laws, but you know who you are.

But mainly thank you to the British, throughout history, for being such wankers.

ABOUT THE AUTHOR

James Felton is a writer and journalist whose articles regularly appear in the *Guardian*, *Independent*, *Daily Mash* and *IFL Science*. As a writer for television, his work includes the BAFTA award-winning 'The Dog Ate My Homework'. Through his Twitter platform of over 100,000 followers and counting, he is a well-known narrator of the Brexit crisis, averaging around 150,000 retweets a month.

NOTES

1 John D. Wright, *Bloody History of London: Crime, Corruption and Murder* (London, 2017), p. 28.

2 Roberta Frank, 'Terminally Hip and Incredibly Cool: Carol, Vikings, and Anglo-Scandinavian England', *Representations* (California, 2007), Vol. 100, p. 27.

3 Soutik Biswas, 'How Churchill "starved" India', www.bbc.co.uk/blogs (accessed 06/06/2019).

4 Madhusree Mukerjee, *Churchill's Secret War: The British Empire and the Ravaging of India during World War II* (New York, 2010), p. 24.

5 Maya Oppenheim, 'Winston Churchill has as much blood on his hands as the worst genocidal dictators, claims Indian politician', www.theindependent.co.uk (accessed 07/06/19).

6 Walter Thornbury and Edward Walford, *Old and New London: Westminster and the western suburbs* (London, 1891), p. 471.

7 Danby Pickering, *The Statutes at Large from the First Year of Q.Mary, to the Thirty-fifth Year of Q.Elizabeth, inclusive* (London, 1763) p. 288.

8 Dr Brooke Magnanti, 'Ladies, would you buy your boss "obligation chocolate" for Valentine's Day?', www.telegraph.co.uk (accessed 06/06/2019).

9 William Ullathorne, *The Devil is a Jackass* (Bath, 1995), p. 118.

10 William Dalrymple, 'The East India Company: The original corporate raiders', www.theguardian.com (accessed 08/062019).

11 John Meurig Thomas, *Michael Faraday and the Royal Institution: The Genius of Man and Place* (Florida, 1991) p. 132.

12 Paul Simons, 'The big stench that saved London', *The Times* (accessed 09/06/2019).

13 Gaurav Desai, *Subject to Colonialism* (Durham and London, 2001), p. 82.

14 Andrew Melrose, *Told From the Ranks* (London, 1897), p. 23.

15 Brendan Graham, 'Historical Notes: God and England made the Irish famine', The *Independent* (accessed 08/06/2019).

16 Susan Snow Wadley, *South Asia in the World: An Introduction* (New York, 2014), p. 41.

17 Colette Flight, 'History – World Wars: Silent Weapon: Smallpox and Biological Warfare', www.bbc.co.uk/history (accessed 16/06/19).

18 Harold B. Gill Jr, 'Colonial Germ Warfare : The Colonial Williamsburg Official History', www.history.org (accessed 16/06/19).

19 'This Alien Legacy', www.hrw.org (accessed 08/06/2019).

20 Ronald D. Utt, *Ships of Oak Guns of Iron: The War of 1812 and the Forging of the American Navy* (Washington DC, 2012) p. 431.

21 Iwan Rhys Morus, *Bodies/Machines* (Oxford, 2002), p. 98.

22 Cahal Milmo, 'Revealed: How British Empire's dirty secrets went up in smoke in the colonies', www.independent.co.uk (accessed 07/06/2019).

23 Ian Cobain, 'Revealed: the bonfire of papers at the end of Empire', www.guardian.co.uk (accessed 07/06/2019).

24 Ian Cobain, *The History Thieves: Secrets, Lies and the Shaping of a Modern Nation* (London, 2016).

25 Milmo, Ibid.

26 Ben Johnson, 'The Pig of War of 1859', www.historic-uk.com (accessed 06/06/2019).